Understanding

BDSM Relationships

Understanding BDSM Relationships

Peter Masters

Copyright © 2012, Peter Masters

All rights reserved. No part of this book may be reproduced or transmitted in any form or by any means, electronic or mechanical, including photocopying, recording, or by any informational storage or retrieval system, except with permission in writing from the author.

Books in the present series:

Understanding BDSM Relationships

BDSM Relationships - How They Work

BDSM Relationships - Pitfalls and Obstacles

Also by Peter Masters:

The Control Book

Look Into My Eyes - How To Use Hypnosis To Bring Out The Best In Your Sex Life

This Curious Human Phenomenon - An exploration of some uncommonly explored aspects of BDSM

Cover art by Peter Masters

http://www.peter-masters.com/

ISBN 978-1-4701-9385-0

Contents

1. Introduction — 1
2. The three pillars of BDSM relationships — 11
3. BDSM and sex — 29
4. Uncomfortable thoughts — 35
5. What a BDSM relationship provides — 43
6. Foundations of a BDSM relationship — 53
7. Compatibility — 79
8. Life aspects — 85
9. People — 91
10. Artists and tinkerers — 125
11. Assembling the pieces — 135

Bibliography — 139

Glossary   **141**

About the author   **147**

Chapter 1

Introduction

For the uninitiated I'd like begin with a few words about BDSM. "BDSM" is a cunningly compact acronym which stands for the terms: Bondage and Discipline, Dominance and Submission, and Sadism and Masochism.

BDSM is about relationships and interactions between people. It's about power, control, dominance, surrender, humiliation, pain, and discomfort. Sometimes, but not always, it's about sex. It is often intense and can involve extreme sexualization or objectification.

People practise BDSM in a variety of places: in their bedroom, around the house or garden, or in specially set up rooms which are often called dungeons due to their connection with pain and torture. They may go to social events where they have the company of like-minded enthusiasts and where they get to indulge their desires either with their own regular partner or with someone else eager to explore some aspect of BDSM. These social events are often simply called play parties because people indulge in BDSM play there.

So far, so good.

But, BDSM isn't just about deliberately setting aside specific times to do things to each other with evil implements. Power, control, dominance, and surrender don't necessarily need special equipment, special furniture, a special location, or even to be really obvious or intense. You don't need to dangle a woman from the ceiling by her nipples or use a giant whip on someone who is chained to bolts on the wall and who is screaming and writhing in agony for it to be BDSM. BDSM can be explored and exercised anywhere and at any time. This can be quite subtle and restrained.

The woman who you sit next to on the bus might not be wearing a bra but instead might have her breasts bound with rope. How would you know? Or a normal-looking guy walking past you on the street may have had a metal cage locked around his balls and cock that morning by his mistress. The cage is designed so that he can pee but can't have an erection. If he's "lucky" the cage will have spikes on the inside. How would you be able to tell if he's wearing one or not? Or someone you know might always seem to be wearing a necklet with a little lock on it. How do you know that this isn't a symbolic way to show that they have a master or mistress in the same way that someone who's married wears a ring? And maybe the guy you just saw shopping at the supermarket was a BDSM slave running an errand for his mistress. Can you tell the difference between him and some other ordinary guy just by looking?

One idea which is often neglected but which is fundamental to BDSM is that, save for a few individuals, it is never done solo.

UNDERSTANDING BDSM RELATIONSHIPS

BDSM is always done with someone else. The idea I mentioned above about BDSM being about relationships and interactions between people is vital. In all the examples I've mentioned so far there has been a second person. Even the woman wearing the rope bra in the bus had to have someone tie her into it and almost certainly that same person will later untie her. It probably wouldn't feel right to her to untie herself.

This idea is also reflected in the terms by which we refer to ourselves. For example, a master and a slave go together. You don't get a master who does masterly things on his own. Instead he has a slave. He needs to have a slave otherwise who is he going to master? A master and a slave are complementary. They complete each other. Similarly, a submissive doesn't busily submit all on her own. She has to have a dominant. And, of course, a top must go with a bottom.

It is the interaction between BDSM partners which both expresses their relationship and which satisfies their wants and needs. Just being a master, for example, or just being a submissive isn't enough. I could stand on a street corner being amazingly and intensely masterly all I want, but without a slave or a submissive it isn't going to mean very much and it may get me some very funny looks. To find excitement and satisfaction you need to engage a partner. A master needs to explore and work with a slave. A submissive needs to be with and open herself up to a dominant.

To appreciate the nature of the relationships between us we need to look beyond scenes and dungeons and examine wider questions of wants and needs, the very large range of different types of possible relationships, and how seemingly ordinary activities and even hobbies can find a place in the world of BDSM when we explore it with a partner.

UNDERSTANDING BDSM RELATIONSHIPS

BDSM is huge and before making my next point I'd like to mention a few more activities to go with the quite small number of examples I've given so far:

- Inflicting pain on your partner or, contrariwise, being tortured by your partner,
- Cutting designs into your partner's skin with a scalpel,
- Being whipped by your partner until your back is raw or bleeding,
- Flogging your partner's back and buttocks with a heavy leather flogger until they're red, raw, and possibly bleeding,
- Caning your partner's buttocks or thighs until they are bright red or bleeding,
- Locking your partner in a cage,
- Teasing your partner,
- Torturing your partner,
- Being humiliated or embarrassed by your partner,
- Dressing or behaving as an animal, such as a pony, dog, or cat,
- Pinching your partner's nipples until they are in agony,
- Using hypodermic needle tips to pierce your partner's skin multiple times—including their genitals and nipples—often creating decorative patterns of needles,

Understanding BDSM Relationships

- Ordering your partner around, or being ordered around by your partner,
- Depersonalisation or objectification—such as being used or treated as if you were a chair, a table, or a foot mat.

But there's something decidedly odd about the activities listed above. If we step back and look at them objectively, none of them really look like fun. You certainly don't find any of them on the list of attractions at the average theme park. Nor, objectively, do any of them really look that appealing, satisfying, or rewarding. But for those readers who have seen the light, the activities and examples I've discussed could be exactly the menu for your next exciting evening or weekend with your partner and you might already be salivating at the thought.

Another odd thing is that while all of this is definitely BDSM, what do they have in common? Except for boobs, what does being dangled by your nipples have in common with wearing a rope bra? And what does pulling a cart while dressed as a pony have to do with being locked in a cage? And how can you compare whipping your partner's back till it's raw and bleeding to trampling on them in your high heels?

Also, BDSM is frequently a hit-and-miss affair for many people. Why does it work for some and not for others? Why are all these activities so powerful for some and so blah or downright off-putting for others?

Why is it that being embarrassed at work in front of your colleagues by your boss is something bad, while being compelled to lick the boots of your partner at home can be the best thing since sliced bread?

Why is being beaten with a stick in a dark alley by someone who makes off with your money something to get totally pissed off about, but being accurately and deftly caned on the buttocks by your partner so hard and for so long that you can't sit down for days without wincing can be an experience to enthusiastically share with your friends over coffee?

Why would you never think of pulling a knife on someone on the street when you actually have a wide range of knives at home which you quite happily "pull" on your beloved partner, readily drawing blood from them as you carve designs into their flesh?

What is it that makes all these otherwise unpleasant or downright excruciating activities so pleasurable and satisfying?

And, importantly, what is it about the person with whom we do these BDSM activities that lets this astounding transformation of suffering or pain into pleasure happen? Is it the person? Is it the relationship we have with them? Is it both?

And, perhaps sadly, why does this magic sometimes stop working?

Being without answers to these questions puts us in a position where we don't actually have any control of our BDSM. This is very weird, even paradoxical, because a lot of BDSM is precisely about taking and using control. But the truth is that when a hoped-for relationship fails, or when an existing relationship falters, many BDSM practitioners don't know what to do to fix it. Often, their only solution is to move on to a new partner and hope that the next relationship works.

I've noted in other writings[1] that there's an air of magic to BDSM. While BDSM is not rocket science, many BDSM folk have no idea what makes it tick. For them, it is simply magic.

---

[1] [MASTERS2008, pp. 4 - 5]

UNDERSTANDING BDSM RELATIONSHIPS

Indeed, using a flogger the right way on the right person can be a powerful or even magical experience. But if you find that waving your magic flogger no longer leads to sub-space or orgasms, or that the magic knots which used to bring so much joy have become merely blah, where do you go and what do you do to fix it? Google? Facebook? Phone a friend? Trial and error?

Understanding BDSM and BDSM relationships means that we can get ourselves out of the situation where we just have to suck-it-and-see and into the situation where we know why some things are effective and some not, why some things stop being exciting or satisfying and how to get them back on the rails again, and how to take control and set about making our BDSM work.

I have a number of goals for this book and its two siblings[2,3]:

1. To explore and explain the nature of BDSM,

2. To examine what people look for in their relationships with their BDSM partner,

3. To point out the reasons why we do the most common BDSM activities,

4. To look at some of the reasons why BDSM relationships fail and at the ways in which they fail, and

5. To look at ways these failures can be prevented.

Unfortunately, some relationships are doomed from day one. Some, in fact, should have prominent red labels attached saying,

---
[2] *BDSM Relationships - How They Work*
[3] *BDSM Relationships - Pitfalls and Obstacles*

Do Not Resuscitate. But others have a chance, and I am hopeful that what I say in these books can assist in making that chance into reality.

No two people do BDSM for the same exact reasons. As I make my meandering journey through the whys and wherefores of BDSM, keep in mind that while some of what you read here may not apply to you today, it may apply to your partner. As you grow and explore, it may even apply to you sometime in the future.

Questions

At this point, I'd like to ask you to stop and reflect on your connection to BDSM. As I mentioned earlier, the subject of BDSM is huge and I'd like you to start thinking about where in this huge space you see yourself.

- How do you see BDSM? What does it mean to you?
- Why do you do BDSM, or why are you interested in it?
- Do you know what can excite you in a scene?
- Is this satisfying in a long-term sense? Do you need anything else from a BDSM relationship?
- If yes, what do you need long-term? How does this differ from what's exciting during scenes?
- If you have a partner, do you know what they desire to get out of their relationship with you?
- Do you know what they need from the relationship?

- What part do you play in getting their needs met?
- If you don't currently have a partner, what will any future partner be getting from you?

And:

- Why are you reading this book?
- What do you hope to get out of it?

Chapter 2

The three pillars of BDSM relationships

In this chapter I'd like to start exploring what we look for between two people which helps us recognise firstly, that they're actually doing BDSM and secondly, what sort of BDSM relationship they have with each other.

Ah ha!, you may exclaim. Isn't actual BDSM obvious? Can't you tell by the rope, the floggers, and the chains? Well, it's true that sometimes you can. If what we're looking at is a BDSM scene occurring in a BDSM dungeon then we can pretty confidently say that this is BDSM. But not all BDSM is done in a dungeon with rope, floggers, and chains. Maybe you see a couple at lunch in a small cafe. The man realises that there's no salt or pepper shaker on their table and he asks his partner to get the pepper and salt from a nearby table. Is this BDSM? It could be. It could be that this couple is a master and his slave having lunch together and that what looked like a request for her to get the salt and pepper was actually an order. In fact, during their lunch together she could be following a strict protocol imposed by him dictating what she can eat, how she can eat, when and how she should speak, and so on.

This brings up an interesting point: even if we do see two people in a dungeon busily doing things with some rope and a handful of floggers, this may not be all there is. Just as something quite powerful can be going on between a master and his slave in circumstances which seem quite innocuous such as a cafe, there might well be something quite intense going on in the dungeon which we can't see. The obvious stuff with the floggers, etc., may not actually be the main event. Underneath the physical displays of prowess with knots and stamina against the heaviest flogging, something else more psychological, emotional, or even spiritual could be going on.

Even if we're sure that there's BDSM going on, how can we tell if what we're seeing is a relationship with a sound, deep, and effective BDSM basis or whether we're just seeing some kinky fun? These questions are important because if we're trying to develop a relationship with a current or potential BDSM partner then we need some idea of the nature of the beast we're dealing with. It's no use, for example, trying to explore the depths of delightful BDSM depravity when all we or our partner are interested in is an occasional kinky sex session with pink, fluffy handcuffs. On the other hand, if we are in a developing relationship which has the potential to be very profound and intense for us BDSM-wise and we approach it with a lack of respect and treat it as light, kinky fun, then we may quickly find ourselves looking for a new partner.

Understanding BDSM Relationships

In this chapter I'd like to suggest that there are two things we can use to recognise effective BDSM, and an additional third which we can use to recognise that two people have a significant BDSM relationship rather than just being two folk doing BDSM together. I call these three things the pillars of BDSM relationships. They provide the solid supports on which any BDSM relationship rests. They are:

- Disparity of power,
- Penetration, and
- Engagement.

2.1 The first pillar: disparity of power

Those of us into BDSM sometimes refer to *vanilla* people or *vanilla* folk or *vanilla* activities. When we talk about vanilla what we're generally talking about is the egalitarian world outside of BDSM where everyone supposedly has equal rights and equal power to direct their destiny.

This is not the world of BDSM.

In BDSM, we often don't talk about husbands, wives, girlfriends, or boyfriends because these don't hint at or suggest anything more than a completely power-balanced relationship. In BDSM, we instead talk about tops, bottoms, masters, slaves, dominants, and submissives. These names or roles have built in to them a distinct idea of who is in charge, who directs or decides, and who follows or submits.

This difference in power usually appears in the form of one person leading or setting the direction for what goes on between the two, and the second person following or being directed. Many people would like to think that this first person is the top, the dominant, or the master, and that this second person is the bottom, the submissive, or the slave. This is not always the case.

There are many ways in which power can be different between two people, and to a large extent the fact that there are a great many ways this power difference can exist or be created is why BDSM is so varied.

A power difference can be innate, or it can be learned, or we can simply choose for it to be so. When power is innate it can be something like physical strength, or a susceptibility to fetish, or a desire or need to control.

When it's physical strength it means that this power can be expressed through manhandling, or by grabbing your partner by the hair and hauling them physically to where you want them, or by physically wrestling them and overpowering them. This can be very primal.

When you have a susceptibility to fetish, instead of having a power to use over someone else, this is a power which can be used over you. If your particular fetish is feet, for example, then your partner has two excellent tools at the ends of his or her legs which they can use to control, inflame, or extinguish your sexual feelings.

And when your own desires or hungers lead you either to take control of your partner or to be controlled by them, then you're moving into dominance and submission where actions can be less important than the intent behind them. Instead of focussing on particular or stereotypical BDSM activities involving rope, whips, or canes, the important thing is that you are decisive and authoritative and use this to direct and control your partner, be it in a dungeon, on the street, or even in a cafe.

Understanding BDSM Relationships

Power can also be learned. In this case, we often call it skill or ability. An ability to tie amazing networks of knots is something that's learned, and it's a skill which you can then use on someone else. Flogging, whipping, piercing, cutting, and a range of other forms of BDSM play are also skills which take practice to learn, after which an endless stream of submissives will beat a path to your door. These skills and abilities are tools which give us power to affect our partner and to which our partner will surrender.

We can even choose when and how power should appear for us to use. If you and your submissive go out to a relatively isolated bit of forest and she is naked then you have created a situation where you, as her dominant, have an exploitable advantage over her. You can humiliate her or make her feel vulnerable and defenceless. You can play psychological games with her such as by saying, "I think I hear someone coming!" It's simply a matter of picking some place or circumstance where one of you has an advantage or the other has a disadvantage. Another example: giving your submissive subtle orders when you're both together with her vanilla friends. This challenges her to obey, but she also feels the need to try not to be embarrassed or exposed by how she must behave towards you. A final example: having your submissive wear a rope harness under their clothes while you're both out in public or while visiting family.

Differences in power can often be subtle. A volunteer at a BDSM demonstration or workshop can be a good example here. An obvious difference in power lies with the demonstrator. He or she has skill, expertise, and confidence which makes them powerful in regards to performing the particular activity he or she is demonstrating. But, less obvious is that the volunteer also wishes the activity done to them. This readiness creates an opportunity for the demonstrator to exert his or her skill or ability on the volunteer. Without this readiness to experience the power of the demonstrator there would be no BDSM at all. The disparity in power isn't just that there is this difference, but also that there's an opportunity to exert it.

Another, perhaps unexpected, choice which can cause a disparity of power is when we create a goal. For example, as a dominant I might decide that I want my submissive to learn how to kneel gracefully. If I am determined about this goal then this determination is a strength or power which I can use. It gives me a drive and a focus which I can direct towards my submissive. Having a goal and choosing to use or involve my submissive in attaining it is something which I can assert and is something to which she can surrender. It is a force within me which I can bring to bear on my submissive, such as in the present example by exercising her repeatedly until her movements are smooth, fluid, and look effortless.

2.2 The second pillar: penetration

Penetration is my second pillar of BDSM. Although it's tempting to think the word refers to sexual penetration, it actually refers to the ability to make your partner feel you. In particular, it's about exploiting or using the difference in power which I discussed above. The fact that there is a difference or inequality in power is not sufficient. You need to use it or experience it. It must be felt. Until you use the power it is only potential BDSM. Going to an isolated area of forest, for example, and undressing your submissive is not going to be powerful or effective unless you do something with this situation to affect both you and your partner.

UNDERSTANDING BDSM RELATIONSHIPS

When a top has a bottom strapped to some diabolical apparatus and is busy flogging them mercilessly, or is dropping molten wax on some sensitive part of their anatomy then, ideally, both of them are getting something positive out of it.

While it's clear that the bottom is getting some serious stimulation via the flogger or the wax, it's not so clear what the top is getting out of it. Indeed, if the bottom is doing an impression of a dead fish and is simply standing or lying there without moving or saying anything, then the top is probably not getting anything at all out of the scene except practice. In fact, life might be simpler for him if he simply sets up a pillow and hammers that instead or blows out the candle and goes to watch some TV.

On the other hand, if the bottom is moving, writhing, moaning, or begging in response to the flogger strokes or the drops, then the top is getting feedback and the bottom is directly stimulating the feelings and responses of the top. The writhing, moaning, etc. cause the top to react and be aroused.

If one or both people involved are not actually feeling something as a result of the actions of their partner, then there is little or no BDSM there for them.

It's easy, for example, for a top at a BDSM party to demonstrate their skills at flogging or caning and for the recipient to have a jolly good time. It might well be though, that the top is not being particularly involved and is instead merely going through the motions for the purpose of the demonstration. Thus there might be BDSM activities going on, but the penetration is only one way. Only the person being flogged or caned is being penetrated. This can happen with an established couple as well, with one person doing the appropriate deeds because their partner wants or needs them without the first partner being involved or excited

The three pillars of BDSM relationships

by it at all. In fact, here we find one of the first ways in which a BDSM relationship can fail, namely lack of involvement when penetration only occurs in one direction.

Penetration can also take other forms. I was at a BDSM party once where a number of the dominants were sitting in a circle talking while their submissives sat at their feet. During the conversation, one of the female dominants decided to make a point by ordering her female submissive to perform oral sex on one of the male submissives. This was notable because of the different forms of penetration involved:

- Firstly, and obviously, the female submissive was orally penetrated and felt the penis of her cohort in her mouth.

- The female submissive was also penetrated by the authority of her dominant who ordered her to perform such a public exercise. In other words, the submissive felt the exercise of her dominant's authority over her.

- The female submissive was penetrated by those of us watching. Certainly the experience would have been less intense for her, and possibly less challenging, had there been no audience. As it was, a number of the dominants made comments thus adding to the penetration and experience of the female submissive.

- The female dominant herself was penetrated by experiencing her submissive responding to her authority, and by seeing how everyone else present responded to what her submissive was doing under her orders.

- Those of us watching were penetrated or effected by the performance.

UNDERSTANDING BDSM RELATIONSHIPS

It is this multiple penetration aspect of BDSM which can make sex hotter. Beyond the feeling of cock-in-cunt (or cunt-enclosing-cock) which gives a purely physical penetration, BDSM allows for authority to be exercised, another form of penetration, and for the use of pain or physical manipulation such as through impact play or bondage, which is an additional form of penetration. This allows BDSM to effectively triple (or more) the different types of penetration occurring during sex thus giving much more intensity.

Using an unequalness in power to penetrate our partner is largely what defines BDSM. Disparity of power alone, or penetration alone don't do it. But using power to create penetration does. This can be a complex and subtle dance. As I mentioned above, a bottom or submissive can and does penetrate their top or dominant. In an impact play scene, for example, they do it with their moans and writhing as they are struck by the cane or whip. In effect, this is a power which the bottom or submissive has over their top and it highlights that even though in a scene it might seem that the top or dominant is nominally in charge, power to affect the other lies with both people involved.

This begs the question: if both people in a scene have power over the other, then doesn't this render the idea of one being a master and the other a slave, or of one being a dominant and the other being submissive, meaningless? This isn't the case. The idea of a top, dominant, or master is that they are the one who leads or who takes charge. It may not necessarily be that they are the ones with all the power, but it is frequently the case that they are the ones who determine when and how the power is directed, be it by them over their partner, or by them creating or allowing situations where their partner can use power over them.

The three pillars of BDSM relationships

2.3 The third pillar: engagement

BDSM is not done solo. Even the aficionados of self-bondage can have an Other present with them when they are practising bondage alone. In their case, where they employ a strategy to prevent themselves from being able to escape—such as by using a combination lock at night thus forcing them to wait until the daylight to escape, or by encasing the key to the final padlock in a block of ice thus requiring them to wait until the ice has melted—this Other is Time. Time compels them to remain restrained, regardless of any protestations they may make, until it is ready to allow their release[1].

However, just because there's another person taking part in a BDSM scene with you doesn't necessarily mean that you have any sort of meaningful BDSM relationship with them. It is important to recognise this difference between simply doing BDSM and being part of a BDSM relationship. Doing BDSM may merely be allowing someone to tie you up and enjoying the embrace of the rope, or can be flogging someone and watching them writhe and see their back turn red. Both of these and other activities may be enjoyable, but don't necessarily mean that you're part of any sort of BDSM relationship.

We could say that a BDSM relationship requires an intimate and personal involvement rather than just a technical involvement. Indeed, the idea of engagement means that what we are doing is interacting with our partners in some form or other and that they are interacting with us. Merely hitting them and seeing them jump is not necessarily such an interaction. You could go around

---

[1] [MASTERS2008, pp. 53 - 54]

hitting all sorts of people and watching them jump but it doesn't mean that you are having a relationship with them.

Engagement is my third pillar of a BDSM relationship. Going to a BDSM party, meeting some cutie, tying her up, flogging her, and being turned on by it is not engagement. She is not engaging us and we aren't engaging her. In fact, we really don't know her from a bar of soap although she may have better breasts. Instead, we are actually engaging ourselves by imagining that she is feeling or thinking in some particular way. We respond to what we imagine she is feeling, not to what she is actually feeling. In other words, while we are performing the physical aspects of our BDSM on her we are actually engaging something conjured up in our own imagination. This something we have in our imagination could perhaps be called the Average Bottom or the Average Submissive. If we do want to play with someone new then we do what we know the Average Bottom likes or what the Average Submissive likes.

The same thing applies to submissives and bottoms who want to play with or impress a top or dominant they fancy. Not knowing this person they do what the Average Top or the Average Dominant likes and hope for the best.

This is an important idea because until we know someone well, until we know what triggers they have, how they feel and respond, and what their own intimate wants and needs are, then we are limited to engaging what we think they want or need and what we think they are feeling, not what they actually want, need, or feel. It may well be that with a lot of experience we can get pretty good at guessing what makes someone else tick, but until we do actually know the real them then we're still only going to be engaging what we think they are, not what they really are.

The three pillars of BDSM relationships

UNDERSTANDING BDSM RELATIONSHIPS

Once we have made the transition from imagining or guessing our partner's BDSM experiences to actually engaging our partner on the basis of their real feelings, needs, and responses then we can have a BDSM relationship with them. Before this point we can't. We might think we can, but the key is knowing them, not thinking that we know them, and not filling in the gaps of what we know with what we'd like to imagine them to be.

When we intimately engage someone else we use our personal knowledge and awareness of their strengths, weaknesses, triggers, emotions, desires, and needs to cause a real, rather than imagined, reaction in them. This is what happens when a top or bottom actively engages his bottom or submissive during play. But this engagement works in both directions. Bottoms and submissives who know their partner well can moan, wriggle, yell, scream, lubricate, get an erection, smile, and wink in ways which intimately impact their top or dominant.

Understanding this is important to the shape of any BDSM relationship you may have.

Consider this: if someone can get their rocks off by flogging anything with breasts and a vagina, then they're not engaging you. Likewise, someone who's deliriously happy to be tied up by anyone who can do knots isn't being engaged by you. They're being engaged by their relationship with the rope. You just happen to be holding it.

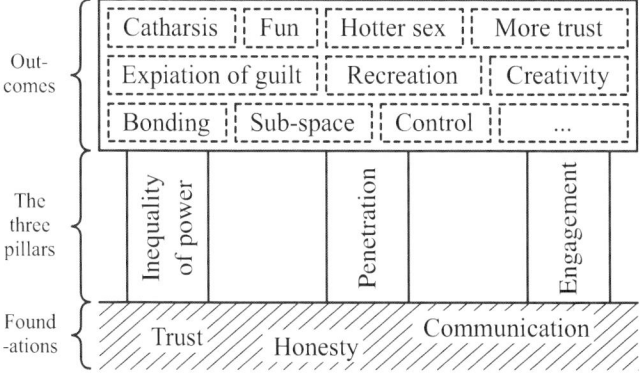

Figure 2.1: The levels of BDSM

2.4 The place of the three pillars

When we step back from BDSM and try to see it in its entirety, we may be able to see it as three levels, each one building upon the other. I've represented these levels in figure 2.1. They are:

1. Foundations
2. Three pillars
3. Outcomes

The foundations will always be trust, communication, and honesty because these provide the solid base which holds up everything else. Without honesty the foundations can become like shifting sands, moving about as circumstances change, and on which nothing substantial can be constructed. Without communication there won't be any relationship because relating is explicitly about communicating. And without trust there will always be barriers and distance which limit or prevent engagement.

On top of the foundations are the three pillars, and resting on top of the three pillars are the outcomes. The outcomes are what we get out of our BDSM. We don't do BDSM because we just want inequality of power, or because we just want penetration, or because we just want engagement. We want what these things give us, where they take us. Take pain, for example. No one does BDSM for the pain. They do it for where the pain takes them, for the state of mind they can achieve through the pain, for the release they get from experiencing intense pain. If someone went into a BDSM scene, experienced a lot of pain, and then finished the scene feeling exactly the way they did when they started, then they wouldn't do it at all. The pain needs to do something, change something, release something. Pain alone, while it might be intensely penetrating, needs to do something useful.

The same applies to rope and bondage. A dominant doesn't tie someone up just for sake of tying. They need to feel some outcome. Maybe their partner ends up feeling super horny and after the scene is ravenously sexual, or maybe the dominant finds that focusing on the fine detail of decorative bondage is relaxing, or maybe they get their own rush from experiencing power over their partner. Whatever the reason, there needs to be an effective outcome from the use of the inequality of power, the penetration, and the engagement, otherwise we don't use them.

There are many things which we look for in our BDSM relationships, many more than the super horniness or relaxation

Understanding BDSM Relationships

I've just mentioned. We could include fun or recreation as an outcome, or greater bonding with our partner, increased trust, and increased intimacy. These are all valid and quite common outcomes, and often they are important parts of building a strong relationship with our partner. There are many more outcomes and in book two of this series I'll be looking at these a lot more closely.

I hope that at this point you can begin to see the structure and the pillars that I've been talking about, particularly in relation to your own BDSM and to the people you share it with.

One of the important things which I've noted elsewhere about BDSM when compared to vanilla relationships, is that in BDSM we do things to our partners or they do things to us. In vanilla-land, we instead do things with partners, not to them. This difference of "with" versus "to" is one of the key things which lets us actually see or define a difference. This goes hand in hand with the first two pillars I mentioned, unequalness of power and penetration, because we use these to do *to* our partners. We don't necessarily need to actually be more powerful in a physical sense, though we can be. More, it is the desire or need to actually use our skills, abilities, strength, desires, or determination to create situations in which we can penetrate our partners and have them feel us doing things to them, and to create situations in which their responses can affect or penetrate us.

These two pillars let us recognise BDSM, but this book and the others in this series are about BDSM relationships and to have a BDSM relationship we need to actually engage the person with whom we do our BDSM. This is the third pillar.

There are lots of things we can consider here. For example, if we have a long-standing friendship with someone and as part of that we satisfy our BDSM needs by, say, tying them up or being

The three pillars of BDSM relationships

tied by them, are we having a BDSM relationship along with the friendship? Or are we merely friends who do BDSM? Can we be friends on one level and have a BDSM relationship on another?

I'd like you to keep in mind that sex isn't necessary to BDSM. In fact, you don't even need to get horny at all and still do BDSM. Is it possible therefore, to have a perfectly satisfying sexual relationship with someone and to separately have a platonic BDSM relationship with that same person?

Considering BDSM in terms of the three pillars I have listed also lets us see a difference between the, er, "classical" idea of a master or slave—such as in the old American South, or in the ancient world—and our present BDSM incarnation of these roles. A classical master used a slave for the service that they received, for the benefit from the slave. It wasn't the act or fact of mastering which was important. It was the service or the utility the slave provided. That was the sole value.

In BDSM terms however, a master doesn't just order a slave around to get service or some utility benefit. They use their slave precisely for the experience they get from doing so, for the penetration they themselves experience. The service can actually be secondary.

Likewise, a BDSM slave or submissive doesn't serve solely to be beneficial to their master. They serve to feel penetrated.

By talking about three pillars, what I'm trying to do is allow us to recognise a BDSM relationship as distinct from some other type of relationship. A relationship doesn't need all three pillars, but without them it isn't BDSM. With them, it is. For example, there doesn't need to be inequality of power for there to be penetration. Someone can be penetrated or strongly affected by the looks, sense of humour, attitudes, or caring nature of their partner. This doesn't mean that there's an unequalness of power being exercised though.

Penetration can be absent in a relationship and this means it isn't BDSM, but it can still be a successful vanilla relationship. As we've seen, BDSM is about doing to rather than with. Two people who enjoy bungee jumping and get an intense rush out of it might spend a lot of time together, know each other's desires intimately, and put a lot of time into planning their bungee adventures, but when it comes down to it, it is the bungee jumping which is doing the penetrating, not the partner.

Even engagement can be missing and two people can still have an entirely satisfactory relationship which they both find rewarding. It just isn't a *BDSM* relationship. For example, two people who backpack the world together may feel comfortable in each other's company, and may share the burden of organising hotels, trains or flights, but they may not actually know much about each other or, indeed, care. The scope of their relationship may merely be as travelling companions and it might be a highly successful one, with them both ending their adventures saying what a fantastic time they had, but it wasn't really with each other even though they both happened to be there at the time.

By understanding the nature of these three pillars we can gain the ability to distinguish a BDSM relationship from other types of relationship. In particular, when we're trying to understand or troubleshoot a BDSM relationship it is often the nature of these three pillars which tells us how that relationship works, what its strengths are, and its vulnerabilities.

Chapter 3

BDSM and sex

There seems to be a great deal of confusion about the nature of BDSM. A lot of people, and I mean A LOT, seem to think it's just about sex. If it were just about sex then this would make many things very easy. Unzip your fly or take off your panties and the BDSM can begin. Zip up your fly or put your panties back on and the BDSM is over. There'd be no need to wonder whether you're crazy or not because you like being tied up or because you like whipping your partner so that they howl and bleed. If BDSM were only about sex you could say that the pain and the rope are just a part of a big sex game and that what you do in your dungeon or your bedroom is not a reflection of who you really are.

It's true that there are many people who use BDSM activities, such as light bondage or flogging, as a sex aid. This includes the countless thousands or millions who use a hint of BDSM for titillation in the bedroom. They may use silk scarves or cheap, fluffy, plastic handcuffs from the local sex-aid shop for bondage, or they may use light, soft floggers for sensual teasing. This is often simply symbolic. The scarves and plastic handcuffs are not robust and can't withstand any real struggling, and the light floggers do little more than suggest pain, but the idea of being tied or flogged can be powerful and may lead to mighty erections and voluminous lubrication. For some people, the fact that it is only symbolic can be very reassuring because the real thing can be, for any of a number of reasons, quite frightening.

It is a very important and very significant step to be able to divorce your BDSM interests from sex. By saying that the pain, the rope, the service, or any of the other aspects of BDSM are important and significant to you just on their own and without sex, you are stepping away from a safe intellectual harbour. You can no longer justify to yourself or to others that what you do is just "kinky sex." But taking this step can be very empowering. It can actually allow you to fully embrace BDSM because you no longer need to maintain a veneer of plausible deniability either for others or for yourself. Trying to believe that your BDSM practices are just about sex can actually hold you back from exploring other areas of BDSM which may be even more rewarding and satisfying for you.

While BDSM isn't necessarily about sex, sex can be a very effective tool to use in BDSM play. As I've already noted, BDSM is about power, control, domination, and surrender. To control, to dominate, or to surrender there must be something powerful involved. Sex can be that powerful thing. I stress that it can be. It need not be sex. Pain is also powerful. Ropes and restraints can be powerful. Even fear can be powerful. All these things are excellent BDSM tools. For the moment however, we're talking about sex.

UNDERSTANDING BDSM RELATIONSHIPS

Making a guy feel horny and then preventing him from having an orgasm can be a very effective use of sex. You might put his cock in a cage with spikes on the inside to torture him so that when his cock becomes erect the spikes stick in. Or you might take a woman, tie her down with her legs apart, and then apply a very powerful vibrator to her clitoris. We could debate the relative merits of no orgasms versus too many orgasms, but suffice it to say that they are both very effective in their own way. They are both tools to create feelings of helplessness or surrender for the submissive, and for the dominant they create feelings of power or of being in control.

Your own BDSM play may involve a lot of sex. There's nothing wrong with that and I'd never suggest that there was. But in this chapter I'm trying to stress that BDSM is not sex, nor is sex BDSM. While there are those folk out there for whom BDSM is merely sexual foreplay, there are also many hard-core BDSM folk for whom their BDSM activities are the goal rather than being merely a warm-up for some hot-'n-horny nude gymnastics. In case your own particular BDSM circumstances make this distinction difficult to see, I'd like to give a few more examples to make my point.

A couple into cutting, where one cuts designs into the other's flesh with a scalpel without the aid of an anaesthetic, don't generally engage in a long session of carving designs into flesh and then suddenly whip off their clothes and get at it. It's often the pain and the artistry which are important for them, and despite what some people might like you to think, it is actually agony and it doesn't necessarily make you horny[1].

---

[1] It is appropriate to note that cutting also can be done so that it involves minimal or no pain. This is the case when the knife is used very lightly to cut

BDSM and sex

In a similar way, a couple into heavy impact play, such as whipping, caning, or spanking, are not going to have a long session where the top puts in every bit of energy he has to hammer his partner with every whip and flogger at his disposal and then, sweat dripping off him and barely able to stand any more, leap vigorously onto his partner (who is feeling similarly exhausted) and have energetic sex. No. More likely they will both curl up somewhere and either rest or fall asleep.

Finally, a guy into suspension bondage with his partner is not going to construct some amazing rope bondage, winch his partner high into the air, then whip off his clothes and start leaping into the air with an erection hoping to fortuitously (and briefly) enter his partner in some satisfying fashion before falling back to the ground.

3.1 BDSM and fetish

There's another bit of sexual mystery which also gets mixed in with BDSM sometimes. It's called fetish. A fetish is an object, thing, or a non-sexual part of the body which atypically stimulates someone sexually. Rubber and latex are common fetish materials; corsets and stockings are common fetish clothes; and feet and elbows are common fetish parts of the body. They become a fetish when these typically non-sexual objects make someone feel sexually aroused.

---

through only the top one or two layers of skin. Oftentimes this form of cutting also doesn't draw any blood.

UNDERSTANDING BDSM RELATIONSHIPS

There's a very important element to this definition of fetish. This is that fetish doesn't need to involve a second person[2]. Remember that with BDSM we always have a second person involved, such as the person tying the knots, the person giving the orders, the person cutting the flesh, or the person wielding the cane.

BDSM differs from fetish in two important ways:

1. BDSM always involves a second person while fetish never does,
2. BDSM doesn't always involve sex while fetish always does.

BDSM can go hand-in-hand with fetish, but it isn't fetish. But because fetish is about causing sexual excitement and because—as we've seen—sexual excitement can be a powerful BDSM tool, it means that fetish can be a powerful tool in BDSM play. If your partner is intensely aroused by latex, then when you wear latex you have something which you can use to control or manipulate your partner. You can arouse them with a caress from your latex-clad hand or stroke between their thighs with your latex-clad foot. Or you can deny them your latex by tying them up and standing just a bit too far away for them to touch or smell you.

Using your partner's fetish means you have sexual power over them. And power is the name of the BDSM game.

---

[2] Or, at least, not a whole person in the case of feet or elbows.

Chapter 4

Uncomfortable thoughts

There are many uncomfortable thoughts and ideas associated with BDSM. I say uncomfortable because they may not sit easily with the things we'd sometimes like to believe, particularly about ourselves. For example, many people can have trouble accepting the idea that:

- They enjoy striking or hurting their partner,
- That their partner enjoys being struck or hurt,
- That they enjoy being struck or hurt by their partner, or
- That their partner enjoys striking or hurting them.

Understanding BDSM Relationships

I suspect that this discomfort is the source of many people's view that "BDSM is about sex" because the idea of two people having sex is socially acceptable. Even in the most conservative of families or societies the need for sex is understood. The need to strike, bruise, cut, or pierce your partner with needles is not. But, if you can dress up this striking, bruising, cutting, and so on as "kinky sex", regardless of how bad the fit, then suddenly it enters the realm of the acceptable. You can say, even to yourself, "Oh, yes! I do BDSM, but it's just another way of doing sex."

However, sometimes the heavier or more intense forms of BDSM play simply can't involve sex. We need to ask what happens when a couple who enter the world of BDSM via fluffy handcuffs start looking for more or heavier BDSM. While at the fluffy handcuff stage, it's easy to call what they do merely "kinky sex". But, once things start to get heavier, and maybe bruising and bleeding start to happen on a regular basis, or when perhaps they start exploring humiliation or a master/slave relationship, then trying to maintain the illusion that it's still just a kinky form of sex becomes much, much harder. At this point one or both of them may experience enough of an internal conflict that the BDSM must stop. Perhaps they simply cannot reconcile what they do to their partner, or what their partner does to them, with what they think a relationship should be. What happens then to their partner if for this partner there is no such conflict?

BDSM in many of its more intense forms can be a challenging idea to accept. Taking the step beyond justifying your BDSM in terms of kinky sex, light fun, simple role play, or merely as "adding variety", can be hard to make. It means accepting that pain, service, controlling your partner, being controlled by them, and other BDSM-type activities are right for you. You actually need to embrace and fully accept these ideas.

This creates a very concrete dichotomy, a division between BDSM being only about sex (and therefore a safe idea), and BDSM being about something else as well as sex (and therefore an uncomfortable idea). There is no grey area between these two positions. It's also a one-way trip to move from the first position to the second. It can require a lot of revisiting of what you thought you knew about yourself as you come to accept the new role which pain, humiliation, and other BDSM experiences have in your life.

Ideally, both people in a relationship either make this step from sex-only BDSM to a wider view of BDSM together, or have already made the step before they get together.

But when one partner has made this step and the other has not, the path ahead can be gloomy. It's likely that there'll be frustration on both sides—one pushing for more, the other pushing for less. There is not necessarily any right or wrong in this. It just simply may be the way it is.

Can this difference be resolved? Perhaps. But like all such issues the answer, if one is to be found, lies in communication and openness. If one partner cannot or does not make that step to embracing BDSM and its intensity, it might easily be that they don't need it as much as their mate. If other aspects of the relationship are satisfactory and rewarding then maybe something can be worked out.

4.1 Tough to swallow

Although maybe still uncomfortable, some of the more well-known BDSM activities, such as flogging or rope bondage, are easier to swallow in this regard than others simply because they are portrayed in TV shows and movies, or because they sometimes bear a passing resemblance to childhood games such as cowboys and indians.

Sometimes though, what our partners are looking for can be intense, even disturbingly so.

I was at a BDSM workshop recently in which cutting was being demonstrated. Although I've mentioned it before, I haven't actually explained what it is. Cutting is a BDSM activity involving using a sharp knife or scalpel to make cuts into the skin of a submissive or bottom. Some people do this to create designs in the form of scars, some do it for the psychological effect—for the fear or apprehension, and some do it for the raw pain.

At this particular workshop, the submissive being cut as part of the demonstration remarked that it was good that she was there at the workshop because otherwise she'd be cutting herself at home. This leads us to one of the rarely spoken, and sometimes uncomfortable truths about BDSM, and that is a connection for some people between BDSM and self-harm.

Self-harm may develop as a coping mechanism depending on a person's external circumstances, or it may become desirable or needed by someone for no obvious reason. Self-harm can sometimes be a symptom of borderline personality disorder (BPD), or of other psychological disorders. Self-harm appears to be more prevalent in younger people, though it can be found in all age groups and both genders. Self-harm doesn't imply suicidal tendencies. The person who does it might only feel the need every few months and otherwise be entirely fine the rest of the time.

UNDERSTANDING BDSM RELATIONSHIPS

There is a clear attraction for those who self harm and BDSM because BDSM often deliberately involves pain. Those seeking pain can find it in BDSM... on a platter, so to speak.

More important for us than why some people seek pain or seek to harm themselves is the simple fact that they do. For them, it is a need. It can involve a lot of embarrassment for them. It is not seen as socially acceptable. It isn't discussed, and the people who do feel the need to cut often do so alone without letting anyone know about it.

When the need is strong, the people who cut tend to cut deeply looking for strong pain. There's a big risk in this, particularly the risk of bleeding out and dying from loss of blood.

We may debate about this, or argue that self-harm is a symptom of some sort of illness, or that it's a poor coping strategy, but whether it is or isn't is not my place to judge. However, I will say that if someone is going to cut or hurt themselves anyway, it's far better for them either to do so when they're with someone, or for them to be hurt by someone who is able to make sure that it doesn't go too far and who is there to render assistance.

This is a good place for BDSM to come into the picture. A BDSM relationship can provide a safe and supportive environment for someone who needs pain. They can get that experience without needing to do it alone. When they are not alone, or when their partner cuts or hurts them, they can get the pain they need with far less risk, and get it with someone to hold them and support them before, during, and afterwards.

A danger here has to do with the difference between enabling and supporting. A friend of mine recently announced that she was going to run a workshop on the spiritual side of cutting and scarification. She had to turn many people away because it was clear that they were simply looking for somewhere to go and cut themselves. They were looking for somewhere where they'd be allowed to, or be given permission to, or even encouraged to cut themselves. They were wanting someone else to take the responsibility.

BDSM isn't about giving up responsibility. Someone who gives up responsibility is a doormat and probably doesn't have a place in any sort of relationship, BDSM or otherwise.

It can be difficult to draw a line between enabling and co-dependency on one side, and being supportive on the other. When we care about someone we might stray too much towards actually creating situations which encourage them to self-harm when better or healthier options exist. Instead of supporting them, we can make things worse. There is a big difference between supporting someone who has a need for pain, surrender, or humiliation on one hand, and cheering them on on the other.

4.2 Positioning ourselves

When we engage in BDSM, a lot of the time the needs, hungers, and desires which surface are not necessarily the sorts of things you can talk about in church or during a game of bowling with the lads. But with our partners—our submissives, our dominants, our slaves, and our masters—what does arise presents us with opportunities to support and encourage our partners, and for them to support and encourage us. It is perhaps a measure of our commitment to ourselves, to our partners, and to our BDSM, how far we go with this.

This brings us to one of the three pillars of BDSM which I mentioned earlier: engagement. If there are ideas, thoughts, or attitudes which come our way in our BDSM explorations with our partner and we refuse to engage those ideas just because they are uncomfortable, then we necessarily limit where we can go and what we can do.

Chapter 5

What a BDSM relationship provides

For two people exploring BDSM, being part of a relationship creates opportunities to satisfy their BDSM wants and needs in a number of different ways.

Firstly, the relationship can create a context in which they can do more things, or experience things more intensely than they could with a casual play partner. By having an ongoing relationship with a partner who has complementary interests to yours—such as when you like being flogged and they like flogging—it means that you have more opportunities to explore and try out new things. You can afford to experiment because if some new technique turns out to be a disappointment one day, your partner will still be around the next day so you can do something different. In casual play, because it might be the only time you play with this person, you have to get it right first time. You don't take chances or try new things. You stick with what you know works, and you don't try to expand your horizons.

Secondly, because of the trust which comes with a longer-term relationship, you can go to more intimate places in your play than you can with a casual partner. You can even take chances with more intense play, knowing that your partner will be around the next morning or the next day so that you can take care of them or so that they can take care of you.

Thirdly, when you're part of a relationship with your BDSM partner, you don't have the need to make each and every scene a complete episode in itself as you do with a casual play partner. With a casual partner you can't be sure they will be around to continue where you left off next time, or if there will even be a next time. Having a regular partner allows you to adopt the view that what you start today doesn't need to end today, but can be open-ended and continue to play out over the next days, weeks, or even months.

Fourthly, the relationship that you have with each other allows you time to develop an awareness of each other's wants and needs, to establish ways of communicating, to develop trust in each other's intentions and abilities, and to develop your own routines and preferences for when you play together. This can be very comforting, but watch out for complacency!

Another thing which an ongoing relationship provides is an opportunity to more deeply explore BDSM. Profound surrender, submission, dominance, and mastery all become possible when you know that your partner is going to be there for you and with you every day. In a scene with a casual partner you can, at best, only superficially explore control and authority. This is because at the end of the scene you both need to walk away with the same control and authority with which you entered the scene. When you have a regular partner, particularly a live-in partner, this is not the case. When you know that you'll be seeing and interacting with your partner multiple times per day, any handing over of control or exercising of authority can quite realistically last for days, weeks, months, or the length of the whole relationship. For example, in such a relationship a submissive can effectively, productively, and completely hand over control of her sexuality and how she expresses herself sexually to her partner. He will be there to use, administer, and exercise that control in the long-term. On the other hand, the best that can happen in a casual scene in this regard is perhaps some orgasm denial for a couple of hours. And keep in mind that when we're talking about sexual control, a period of only a couple of hours is extremely short when we consider that sexual arousal and sexual tension can be held and built for days with some people.

You can see here that I'm talking about both penetration and engagement, the second and third pillars of BDSM relationships which I discussed in chapter 2. Having trust in your partner and knowing that your activities aren't confined to a simple evening's entertainment together means that you can develop and explore more intense and profound forms of BDSM, and this means more penetration. In casual play, you simply can't go too deep. Casual play might involve intensity, but not depth.

In addition, having a longer-term knowledge of, and experience with your partner builds engagement. Instead of being limited to doing what works for most people—and hence, what will probably work with your partner-of-the-moment—you can learn your actual partner's actual buttons and triggers. You can learn what they respond to and what they need, and then you can engage the Real Them and not an Average Partner.

Understanding BDSM Relationships

5.1 Particular explorations

I'd like to spend a few words here talking about some particular BDSM activities and how they are affected by whether they are performed in the context of a relationship or whether they are just done casually at a play party or just with someone who is only an occasional play partner.

Bondage

Bondage is very much a scene-based activity. This means that bondage lends itself well to being rolled out for quick and casual scenes either at parties or when you're with BDSM acquaintances. These can be rewarding in themselves because for some bottoms and submissives the effect of the embrace of the rope, even if just for 15 or 20 minutes, can be quite intense. Likewise, some tops enjoy the challenge and concentration involved in creating the initial tie and are then happy to move on.

For two people in a longer-term relationship however, more profound and intimate explorations can occur. For example, the top can put his partner into a rope harness over which she wears her normal street clothes for the day.

In addition, studies have shown[1] that bondage can have strong, positive, physiological effects—such as deep relaxation, feelings of floating, and emotional release—which are more easily experienced in a safe and secure environment with someone you trust.

---
[1] [MASTERS2008, pp. 103 - 105]

Bondage also has its intimate side, and being tied up—particularly while naked—can create intense feelings of exposure and vulnerability. Indeed, you can be extremely exposed, vulnerable, and helpless in bondage, and the security of being in a relationship with your trusted partner can allow you to fully surrender yourself into this experience. In a casual scene at a play party or with someone who is merely a BDSM acquaintance, you might leave your clothes on for the bondage for security reasons and thereby lose out on the experience of sexual vulnerability or exposure.

Catharsis

Catharsis is a release of built-up emotional energy in response to something intense, dramatic, or powerful. The events or emotions which cause the initial build up of energy may have no relationship with whatever triggers their eventual release. For example, the built-up energy could come from something that happens at work—something positive, such as a promotion, or something negative, such as irritation with a colleague—which you can't fully let out of your system while you're in a staid working environment and while you're wearing a suit. The energy build up could also come from something that happens with family or with friends, or from something that happens while you're out and about.

When you don't have the opportunity to let those feelings out at the time, you need to find some other opportunity later. This is called catharsis. A trigger for the release of this pent-up energy can be found in some BDSM play such as heavy flogging, cutting, whipping, and humiliation, all of which can be—even just to those watching—quite dramatic and intense.

What a BDSM relationship provides

Understanding BDSM Relationships

While floggings are sometimes handed out at BDSM events and parties with the same readiness as canapes, cheese, and biscuits, the more profound and satisfying experiences leading to catharsis come when two people who know each other take the time to develop such a scene in full awareness of each other's needs.

For example, the common attitude that BDSM equals sex often means that a flogging from Master Gregory The Brutal at a BDSM party will include some gratuitous fondling and heavy breathing. This can seriously detract from a submissive's emotional release when he is actually looking for some regular and heavy thudding into which he can allow himself to sink for ten or fifteen minutes.

This is not to say that a good flogging can't lead to some serious and satisfying nookie, but this works best when the two people concerned do so in the context of a longer-term relationship. Intimacy and long experience with a play partner means that limits are familiar and that the buttons which can be pushed are well known. This means greater intensity and less need for caution. Importantly, it also means that when you do play with your partner you can afford to say, "This scene is for catharsis, and later tonight we'll go for the nookie." Many people engage in BDSM scenes for the cathartic or cleansing effect which intense BDSM can have. This is far easier to achieve with a familiar partner in a familiar context than on a casual basis with a casual partner because you have the time and the opportunity to focus on one set of wants or needs in one scene, knowing that your partner will be around for a different scene later on when you'll be exploring other wants and needs.

Guilt

Not all BDSM is about having a good time. Some BDSM is about making a bad time less bad. Guilt fits into this "less bad" category. For reasons beyond the scope of this book, some people carry a burden of guilt around with them. This is not to say that they've just robbed a bank or stolen candy from a baby. Instead, what I'm talking about is the guilt which for some people stems from childhood, from their upbringing, from their family, or even from their religion. It's either there all the time, or it builds up depending on what's going on in their lives. The archetypal way of dealing with this in a BDSM context is through a spanking—especially in a schoolroom scenario—but any sort of discipline-type activity can serve the same goal. This includes caning, being locked up, being spoken to sternly, and so on.

People don't generally go around telling anyone who'll listen that they feel guilty, need a good spanking, and then ask would this person help them out. Punishment and discipline work best when there is a foundation of trust and a longer-term relationship, and where the "guilty party" can be open and honest about how they feel, and about the sort of discipline, pain, or punishment which they need, for how long, and how intensely. This has some similarity with the point I made above in regards to catharsis. Sometimes, perhaps often, a scene will have a functional purpose beyond mere pleasure and it needs to be recognised as such. If BDSM play is sometimes used to mitigate guilt or to trigger catharsis, this is more easily done in the context of a relationship where you can devote whole scenes to this openly, knowing that there will be scenes at other times for other wants and needs, and that it won't always be about catharsis or guilt.

Cutting

Some activities are, by their very nature, quite intimate. Cutting is one of these and it necessarily involves close personal contact. This can be contrasted with, say, flogging which inherently involves far more physical distance between the top and the bottom. Because of the closeness required for cutting, and because it is often performed on parts of the body which are usually private, some form of trust and respect between the cutter and cuttee is needed. This is easier to come by when there is a relationship underpinning the whole deal.

This doesn't mean that cutting can't be done on a casual basis, but it does mean that the cutter and cuttee are likely to be able to immerse themselves in the intimacy and profundity of the scene far more when they know each other well, than when they are ships passing in the night.

Play involving power

Established relationships also lend themselves to unplanned and spontaneous power play. Even when there's no actual long-term exercising of control or authority going on, such as that which I discussed at the beginning of this chapter, a dominant and a submissive who have a long-term relationship can enter into role either for some playful fun or for something more serious whenever the mood takes them. A good foundation of intimacy, honesty, and trust means that any overture by one—such as the submissive kneeling at her partner's feet, or the dominant grabbing his partner by the scruff of the neck—can be either accepted by the other and lead into something more intense, or can be politely and safely deferred until a later time.

Endorphins

The human body reacts in different ways to prolonged and intense pain. In some cases, it tries to deal with it by releasing neurochemicals which allow us to continue to function in spite of the pain. Some of these chemicals create a "high". This can be a feeling of detachment, for example, or withdrawal. It can also be a feeling of intoxication.

Whatever it is though, it leaves us vulnerable, and while we're in this vulnerable, intoxicated, neurochemically-impaired state, we need a partner who'll watch over us and take care of us until the chemicals have faded away and we're back to what passes for normal. And, again, this is going to be safest, and we're going to be able to surrender ourselves most to such an experience, when we have a trusted, long-term partner with us.

Continuity of context

Continuity of context means that any situation, state of mind, or role which is entered into can continue through to a safe completion. BDSM between casual partners often has less of a guarantee of continuity than BDSM in a longer-term relationship. This is because there is a lack of certainty that attitudes, roles, thoughts, or situations will be picked up from where they left off with a casual partner. Because of this, it often happens that casual BDSM play leaves one or both of the people involved feeling like there has been a lack of closure, that something was missed out on. It can also leave them feeling quite alone.

Combined with the development of intimacy and trust, this idea of continuity is one of the main things which distinguishes

BDSM in a relationship from casual BDSM play. It allows roles to be established, built up, explored and exercised over extended periods and to greater levels of satisfaction than is possible in casual BDSM. Something unfinished in one scene can be picked up in the next and there's no need for fear or concern that this opportunity won't occur.

Chapter 6

Foundations of a BDSM relationship

BDSM is many different things to many different people. For some people it is about pain, for some it is about sex, for some it is about bondage or confinement, for some it is about surrender or profound submission, and for others it is about fear, embarrassment, or humiliation. Some people see it as the focus of their lives, some see it as a sort of hobby, and some see it merely as a kinky adjunct to their sex lives. Because of the large difference in levels of interest in BDSM, and because of the wide range of possible BDSM activities, it follows that the sorts of relationships in which we get involved are also many and quite varied.

This can make it difficult to work out exactly what we are looking for from BDSM. In part this is due to a natural tendency to look at what people are doing around us, compare ourselves to them, and simply imagine what it'd be like if we were doing what they're doing. But, when we examine the sorts of relationships other people are having, what we see might be entirely different from what is going to work for us. These other people might be having entirely reasonable and profoundly satisfying BDSM experiences; they are just going about it in a completely different way from what we might need. This can lead us to doubt ourselves or question whether we're on the right path.

There are however, many right paths and we might just need to find our own.

A challenge to finding our own personal flavour of BDSM is that what we might call mainstream BDSM tends to embrace only a small portion of what BDSM has to offer. When we look at what other people are doing or what is going on around us, we necessarily only see a very, very small subset of all of BDSM. If we look at the folk around us for inspiration they may indeed be practising a variety of interesting styles of BDSM, but the one which would work best for us might not be among them.

This can be a big problem because without having seen, heard, or read about particular approaches to BDSM, it can be hard or even impossible to think them up yourself. The one which is perfect for you might be out there just waiting for you to notice it and start doing it.

In this chapter, I want to present to you a variety of different ways of thinking about BDSM relationships. If you haven't yet worked out what's right for you, these may give you a clue, and if you already have something which works, the ideas here may help you make it better.

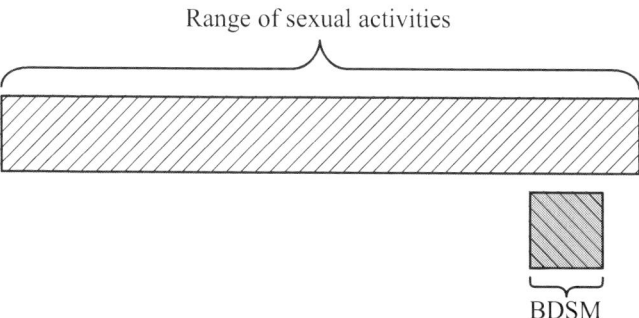

Figure 6.1: BDSM as a small subset of sex

6.1 The quantity of kink

Some people see BDSM primarily as an extension of their sex lives. They view it as kinky sex, or sometimes just "kink". For them it might be that BDSM is strictly a clothes-off activity which always starts or ends with sexual intercourse. This doesn't mean that BDSM equals sex. It means that BDSM is a type or flavour of sex. Figure 6.1 represents this view of BDSM. For such a kinky person, their range of sexual activities includes everything they do with BDSM. It means that they don't see, and sometimes can't even imagine, BDSM without sex.

I've drawn the box representing BDSM activities quite small. For some people it could be smaller, for some people it could be that the BDSM proportion is much larger. When we start considering the sorts of relationships in which BDSM is such a subset of sex, one of the things we can look at is what this proportion is. In effect, this means that we try to determine how much of the sex is vanilla and how much is kinky.

Foundations of a BDSM relationship

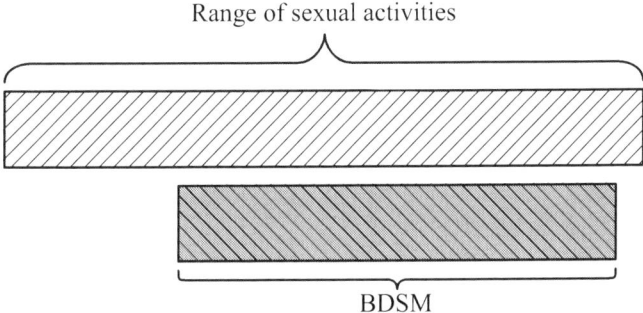

Figure 6.2: BDSM as a large subset of sex

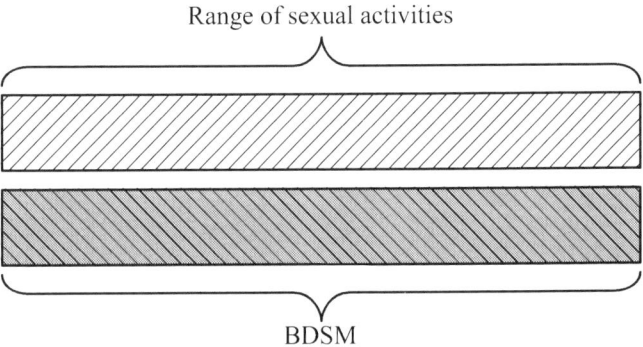

Figure 6.3: BDSM is sex and sex is BDSM

UNDERSTANDING BDSM RELATIONSHIPS

When we look at the sorts of relationships this can involve, one simple way of categorising them is the degree to which kink is involved such as:

- Vanilla with a touch of kink (the BDSM proportion is very small - figure 6.1),
- Mostly kink with a touch of vanilla (the BDSM proportion is very large - figure 6.2), or
- Kink exclusively (sex is BDSM - figure 6.3).

Importantly, these categories will significantly determine which wants and needs can be satisfied for the people involved in them.

For example, someone who is looking to regularly experience intense pain or profound submission during sex is probably going to want to be in a mostly kink relationship. If they're with someone who is looking for a mostly vanilla relationship with just a bit of kink every now and then, then this want or need for pain or submission is probably not going to get met to the extent they need.

Conversely, someone who is only into the occasional use of fluffy handcuffs is going to be best suited for a relationship which is mostly vanilla. They would probably be overwhelmed with a partner who is looking for 100% kink.

Let's look a little closer at these categories and see how the relationships might shape up.

Vanilla with a touch of kink

When a kinky relationship is mostly vanilla, the BDSM elements will only appear now and then. BDSM may just be used to make sex more exciting or adventurous. Perhaps sex with BDSM will simply become part of the couple's sexual repertoire along with sex in a glass-walled elevator, sex in a forest, sex while swimming in the ocean, sex while riding an elephant, and sex while skydiving. It's just another situation or context in which to have sex.

When a relationship is mostly vanilla, the people involved refer to themselves in mostly vanilla terms—such as husband, wife, boyfriend, girlfriend, lover, etc. They don't see themselves in BDSM terms.

Because the BDSM side of their relationship is a subset of the sexual side, and because most people don't fuck 24 hours a day, 7 days a week, this means that the BDSM aspect can be separate from and still coexist with other aspects of the relationship between these two kinky folk.

They could be friends (or "friends with benefits") who have a friend-type relationship including sex and occasionally some BDSM. They may engage in BDSM casually, or sometimes at play parties, or in the privacy of one or the other's apartment or home.

It could be that one or both have mild BDSM and sexual needs and they recognise this. It might be that these needs aren't strong enough to support a long-term live-in relationship and they just get together nookie-wise as needed.

Alternatively, they could actually be lovers. They could live together or just date. Sex is common or frequent, and sometimes it involves BDSM.

They could be married, and with this level of commitment to each other, they might have decided to invest in equipping a dungeon in their basement with all the paraphernalia they typically use in their BDSM sessions.

One of the important features of this type of relationship is that it's scene-based. The BDSM shenanigans, like most sexual activities, have a clearly defined start and end, and once they've ended the couple go back to being vanilla.

Mostly kink with a touch of vanilla

Some couples like a lot of kink, and they like it to add flavour to much of their lives. In other words, it leaks out of their bedrooms and they allow both it, and references to it, to colour their lives in general. Because the BDSM aspect is often a focus, they may think of their partner in BDSM terms—such as being their dominant, submissive, master, mistress, slave, etc. This may be some or most of the time.

In contrast to those people for whom BDSM plays a minor part in sex, these kinky folk will often see their sexuality in terms of BDSM. But, like their less kinky counterparts described above, they won't be doing it 24 hours per day, seven days per week.

They might be two kinky people who get together almost solely to get their kinky needs met. Again, this could be because that their kinky needs aren't enough to support a long-term committed relationship. They could be a top/bottom or dominant/submissive couple who don't live together, but who get together from time to time to play and fuck, and who maybe also do non-sexual things together occasionally, such as have coffee or go to the movies. They might have other people in their lives who they also fuck vanilla-wise, but when the two of them are together it is almost always BDSM.

Foundations of a BDSM relationship

Or they could live together in a partnership or marriage. They would be a top/bottom or dominant/submissive couple who share a life together, who live together and who play regularly. Their sex is almost always with a BDSM flavour.

Kink exclusively

When two people have a relationship where sex and BDSM can't be separated at all then it really only matters whether they have anything else together.

If all they ever do together is have sex/BDSM then that pretty much defines the relationship. In this case, you couldn't say that they even have a friendship. Although they may completely trust and respect each other, they may not have any common activities or interests except for their sexual and BDSM adventures.

On the other hand, they could be "friends with benefits", in which case the benefits are always sex with BDSM.

Also, they could be married or they could be life partners. In this case, their sex is always about BDSM.

Compartmentalising

It's important to keep in mind that we're talking about sex here. When you always see BDSM in terms of sex then it makes compartmentalising it easy. Some people like this. It lets you define a simple boundary between BDSM and the rest of your life. If there's no sex then there's implicitly no BDSM.

It also makes managing BDSM simple. If the BDSM side of things breaks down then it isn't your whole life which is affected.

If you're one of those folk who strongly links sex and BDSM then a breakdown in your BDSM activities may affect a large chunk of your sex life, but the rest of your life will continue on. And if BDSM is only a kinky adjunct to an already-varied sex life, then the BDSM, if and when it stops working, can be put aside—temporarily or permanently—with no major loss.

It's worth pointing out that actual sexual intercourse, exactly like many BDSM activities, is scene-based. It has a start and an end, and this makes it really, really easy to combine with scene-based BDSM.

The vanilla folk

When we consider vanilla relationships, factors which contribute to their success typically include:

- Shared and common interests,
- Similar tastes in music, entertainment, food, or sport,
- Complementary sexual needs and desires,
- Aligned political and religious attitudes,
- Shared interest in raising a family, and
- Same taste in friends.

All of these are things which you can find in advertisements by vanilla singles who are looking for long-term partners. Success in such a relationship may be considered to be a measure of peaceful longevity, of how long the people involved remain together and continue to find the sharing of their lives to be rewarding.

A closer look

I don't want to dwell too much on the vanilla side of relationships because it's both beyond the scope of this book and because there are already numerous books and TV shows which deal with them in more than sufficient and sometimes prurient detail.

Instead, I'd like to look now at what do we get if we only consider relationships when viewed from the BDSM perspective?

6.2 When BDSM doesn't mean sex

While some people view BDSM in terms of sex and consider what they do to be merely kinky variations on sex, there are also people who explore BDSM separate to sex. They still may bonk each other senseless after some BDSM scenes, but at other times they explore the BDSM for the sake of BDSM and not for sex.

Having this awareness that for them BDSM and sex may overlap (figure 6.4 on the facing page) but aren't the same changes their perception and experience of any relationships they have in which BDSM plays a part.

Separating out sex from BDSM (figure 6.5) both increases the range of possible activities and relationships they can have, and at the same time tends to increase their complexity and richness.

In particular, once detached from sex and its private, one-on-one, scene-based nature, the BDSM aspect of a relationship can be extended beyond the time constraints of a scene, out of the privacy of the bedroom, and into many other aspects of life.

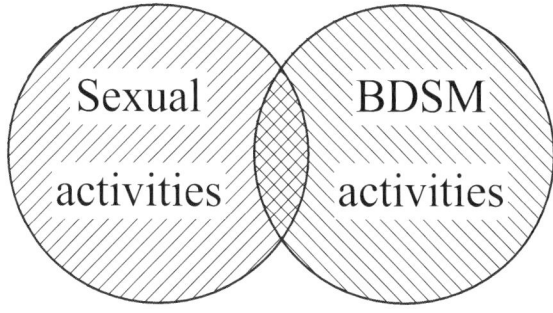

Figure 6.4: BDSM and sex overlap

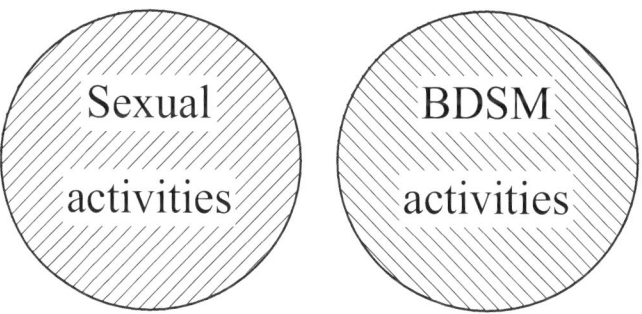

Figure 6.5: BDSM and sex with no overlap

Full-time relationship, full-time BDSM (24/7)

"24/7" BDSM refers to a BDSM relationship which maintains its BDSM flavour 24 hours per day, 7 days per week, 365 days per year.

Some people claim such relationships can't exist. I can understand this point of view because for someone who is into the straight, physical side of BDSM—such as flogging or bondage—it's pretty clear that the flogging must stop from time to time if only due to exhaustion or because bruises and abrasions need time to heal. In fact, any sort of BDSM based solely on specific physical activities—cutting, piercing, humiliation, erotic denial, etc.—has to stop from time to time and so can't be 24/7.

Having said that, it becomes clear that 24/7 BDSM—if it can't be based on particular activities—must be based on something else. That something else is attitude. For example, even a mere inclination towards staying full-time in a submissive or dominant attitude with your partner can become a powerful and ever-present component in a relationship when it is recognized and embraced by both people involved.

BDSM doesn't need to be only about activities or scenes which have a clearly defined start and a clearly defined end. For some BDSM couples, the exercise of power, authority, and control is their thing and it plays out in a D&s[1] or M/s[2] relationship between them. This is much less a set of activities and more a set of attitudes and behaviours. When one person—the slave

---

[1] Dominant and submissive
[2] Master/slave

or submissive—has given up authority over themselves to their partner, this context of deliberately imbalanced power can be a 24/7 constant awareness and experience.

Even when they're not with their partner, a slave or submissive can feel the bonds their partner or their relationship has placed on them in terms of tasks or duties to perform, acceptable behaviour, priorities, and allowable choices. These can include how to dress, how to behave towards others, when to be home, what to eat, what to buy, and so on. The slave or submissive knows that they have a partner above them, and they are constantly aware of the position of service they hold. They know that their partner may, at any time, get in contact and give them directions which they must follow.

The master or dominant is just as much a part of this "24/7-ness" as they plan for and take advantage of the behaviour of their submissive or slave partner. In the same way that their submissive/slave partner is aware of the bonds in place on them, their dominant/master is aware both of the bonds they have placed and of the service their partner is performing even when the two of them are apart.

Perhaps we can consider this in terms of actual rope bondage. A submissive who is tied is going to feel the restraint when she moves or struggles. This is the power her dominant partner asserts over her. But even when she is lying there and the embrace of the rope is merely holding her in place, she has the awareness that she is bound. Likewise, a dominant who has delightfully tied his partner isn't going to suddenly cool once the last knot is in place. His pleasure from the bondage continues while his partner is restrained, even just from knowing that his handiwork is having its effect on her.

Foundations of a BDSM relationship

Full-time, 24/7 BDSM tends to best exist when the people concerned are living together or are frequently in each other's company. This is no different to a vanilla full-time relationship where constant presence—such as waking up in the same house in the morning and going to bed in the same house in the evening—is the norm. This provides the time needed for the two people involved to stay on the same track together. Too much time apart allows for one to drift onto a different path to the other.

Full-time relationship, scene-based BDSM

Not everyone is looking for the intensity or immersion that 24/7 dominance and submission or mastery and slavery requires. BDSM folk can be married or live together and not have the same 24/7-type relationship as discussed above.

Many people, in fact, are happy to have a relatively vanilla relationship with just a hint of BDSM, perhaps combined with occasional BDSM scenes which may be quite intense. These people might have BDSM-type decorations scattered around their house or apartment, socialise with other BDSM folk and share war stories about the sub that got away, but their actual BDSM engagements only take place at set times, possibly in a custom-built dungeon in a spare room, or in the main bedroom on the nights when a private box of toys is opened and the chains, ropes, and floggers come out.

The sort of BDSM we're talking about here is scene- or activity-based and it will typically happen when both people involved feel a need. There's a clearly defined start and end to the activities, and when it's all over the toys get put away and the people involved return to "normal" until the next scene.

The advantage of this type of relationship is that any BDSM-related wants or needs can be met when and as required because the two people concerned are available to each other all the time.

This contrasts with a 24/7-type of BDSM relationship where BDSM would colour or infiltrate every aspect of their lives. For those without such a strong need, having a full-time partner to share in the vanilla side of life—such as work, family, movies, theatre, zoo, and holidays—means that each person can do their own thing when they want, do vanilla things together when they want, and tie and flog each other when they want.

Part-time relationship, some BDSM ("friends with benefits")

An interesting term has arisen in modern social life, and that is "friends with benefits". This is a friendship which includes sex and it is something I mentioned a few pages back. It is about two people who care about each other as friends, and who trust each other enough to go to bed together knowing that it's not going to lead to awkwardness such as unwanted talk of marriage or having to meet the parents.

BDSM has the same phenomenon. In this case, it is two people who are friends or good companions and who enjoy a healthy BDSM scene together from time to time. Importantly, they know that their friend/partner isn't going to start clinging to them and isn't going to want to set up a dungeon-for-two.

On the negative side (at least in terms of BDSM), there is the risk that one of the people involved might set up house with someone else and the "benefits" consequently cease for their previous partner.

Foundations of a BDSM relationship

Another problem is that even if they are both unattached, they are likely living separate lives and the opportunities for them to scratch each other's itches might not be so easy to arrange as in 24/7 or living-together relationships.

Part-time relationship, only scene-based BDSM

Then there are the people who get on well in a scene-based BDSM context but who tend not to have any shared interests or desires to see each other when floggers or rope aren't in play.

While it might sound like these folk have very limited opportunities, this can actually include the same sort of thing we see with people who belong to car clubs or who go to science-fiction conventions. This can be social, or intimate, or both, and may involve meeting for lunch or dinner with other like-minded BDSM folk.

These encounters can provide opportunities to let the BDSM side of your personality out for some fresh air with others who happily talk about and share the same BDSM interests. When the socialising is done, BDSM scenes can follow.

This socialising can occur in public cafes or restaurants, in someone's private home (often with BDSM toys or dungeon available), or on specially-planned weekends away with like-minded enthusiasts.

A narrower aspect of this type of relationship includes the people who get together just to scene for their own mutual satisfaction. They may have met at a BDSM party or social event, decided they had similar BDSM interests, and arranged to meet again afterwards for some extra activities.

A variant on this latter type of relationship can be what you get with professional BDSM services where visits are paid for and the goal is strictly a BDSM encounter.

Party-only or scene-only BDSM

While some folk in a relationship might attend and scene at BDSM parties as a couple, some people go to BDSM parties strictly for no-strings BDSM play. They might make themselves available as a demonstration bunny for a workshop on bondage, or as a human torch during a fire play show-and-tell. Or, alternatively, they may take a bag of rope and offer to tie up all comers.

The point is that they can stretch their BDSM "muscles" a bit at the party, and then walk away at the end with their want or need met and with no strings left attached.

One-way BDSM and professional BDSM

The BDSM part of some relationships is strictly one-way. The situation where a person visits a professional BDSM dominant, dominatrix, or submissive, pays their money, and gets what they need, is a good example of one-way BDSM. This is not to say that the professional isn't also getting something out of the engagement, but the obligation is on the professional to satisfy their customer's needs. It's not mutual as it is in other relationships.

Some non-professional relationships can also be one-way in BDSM terms. A case in point can be where someone has BDSM wants or needs which aren't as frequent or as strong as their partner's. This may involve BDSM play when you aren't in the mood. There's nothing wrong with this. Taking care of your partner can be a natural part of a caring and supportive relationship. As long as this is balanced overall and there's no resentment then it's fine.

The previous paragraph refers to BDSM which is one-way only some of the time. This has more of a chance of succeeding than BDSM which is one-way all the time. This can happen when one person loses interest in BDSM (for whatever reason) or where one person never has had any BDSM interest but the two of them are together for other reasons—such as other common interests, children, etc.

6.3 The needs or wants which get met in a relationship

When two people have a relationship involving BDSM, there are two ways that their BDSM wants or needs get met:

1. The relationship itself satisfies the wants or needs. This happens where the relationship involves dominance and submission, or mastery and slavery, and the actual exercising of the relationship—such as the use and experience of power, authority, and control—provide the satisfaction to the people involved.

2. The relationship provides a context in which wants or needs are explored and satisfied. For example, a couple who use flogging as a sort of cathartic release on weekends, or as a lead-in to kinky sex, have a relationship

which creates a safe context in which to engage in flogging.

There can be significant overlap between the above two ways in which needs are met. For example, a couple who have a significant D&s element in their relationship might also use flogging, bondage, cutting, piercing, etc., to satisfy other needs while still staying within the dominant/submissive context.

The relationship itself satisfies want or needs

Sometimes there won't need to be ropes, floggers, leather outfits, dungeons, chains on the wall, or any other obvious signs of BDSM-in-progress for a couple to have an entirely satisfying BDSM relationship. Sometimes it can be the nature of the relationship itself, rather than what goes on inside it, which is satisfying.

This will mostly happen when an important aspect of the couple's relationship has to do with the experience of power; i.e., one person experiencing or exercising power over their partner while their partner experiences power being asserted over them. This can happen in a number of ways. Some of these are obvious, and some not so obvious.

It's obvious when one partner takes the role of dominant or master and then explicitly takes control of, and gives orders and directions to their submissive or slave partner. This can be made extremely evident by the clothes that each wears—or doesn't wear, in the case of a slave or submissive who is kept naked by their partner. In addition, the way each talks to the other—such as the use of "Sir"—makes concrete the sort of relationship they

Foundations of a BDSM relationship

are involved in. The control-taking in this sort of relationship is overt and may even be aggressive.

It's less obvious when the control-taking is more subtle and less imperative. A situation where a dominant provides firm guidance and direction for their naturally-yielding, submissive partner can be perfectly rewarding for some BDSM folk and there may not be any outward sign that BDSM is involved. Such a situation might be where they're both in the car and the submissive is driving. Along the way, the dominant might always choose the route. Or they might go out to dinner together and the dominant always chooses the restaurant. He might even choose and order the meal she eats. There may not be any special clothes or ways of addressing each other in their relationship, but the power and control can be just as pervasive and satisfying for them both.

Power can also be less obviously experienced through teasing, tickling, taunting, or tantalising. That this is BDSM becomes apparent when it's not done out of malice or meanness, when it's almost always one particular partner on the receiving end, and when both see it is a positive aspect of their relationship. This can be a rewarding form of attention which the dominant is happy to give and to which the submissive is happy to surrender. This sort of play reinforces the role or rank which each has in the relationship, and these acts of reinforcement—such as tickling or teasing—are a subtle, but often quite effective, exercise of power.

Service-based relationships can also be powerful BDSM experiences, even without any orders or commands being given by the dominant. While service can be based on a slave or submissive obeying the explicit orders of their partner, in many cases a submissive or slave can fully submit to the desires or wants of their partner without them. All it needs is that their dominant clearly expresses his or her preferences, values, and priorities. This automatically creates a framework for the submissive in which they can direct themselves while still being under the control of their partner.

As an example, a master may have strong ideas about how he wants things done around his house. Once his submissive partner knows these, she can fully surrender to them and provide useful service to him even though he might not have once given her an actual order. The sorts of things he might say are, "I like my bed sheets changed weekly, the house dusted from top to bottom twice a month, and dinner on the table by 6:30pm." He won't be saying to his submissive, "Scum-of-the-earth, prepare my dinner!" or "Slave! Change the bed sheets!" Instead, she has a framework or structure in which she is able to conform to his wishes and desires without the need for explicit orders.

This can work very well for couples where the submissive or slave partner has a background where actually being submissive was frowned upon—such as if they were brought up by a women's liberation mother or in a feminist household. She can submit to her master's wishes and desires while still not being told what to do!

What I have been talking about here effectively creates a 24/7 relationship.

The relationship provides a context

I'd like to spend a few words now talking about topping and bottoming, and about how they change depending on the nature of the relationship between the two people involved.

Foundations of a BDSM relationship

UNDERSTANDING BDSM RELATIONSHIPS

Topping and bottoming usually refer to scene-based BDSM activities, i.e., to activities which have a clearly defined start and end such as a bondage scene, a flogging scene, or a cutting scene.

At first glance, we might think that what's important about these very physical activities is how well they are executed technically, about the aim of the person wielding the flogger, about the firmness of the knots and the layout of the rope by the person doing the bondage, or about the steadiness of the hand of the person doing the cutting. It's true that these are important, but what is often neglected is the people factor.

We can see this people factor when we compare the differences between doing one of these scenes at a BDSM play party with someone we might know only casually, and doing the same scene at home with someone who we know well.

At a play party with a casual acquaintance, the scene needs to be strictly self-contained. There can't be any overrun because this person we're with is not going to be around for much time after the scene ends. We, and the scene, are limited by their availability. Not just by their physical presence or not, but also limited by their ability or willingness to be supportive. With a casual topping or bottoming partner we need to be self-contained ourselves. We often can't lean emotionally on the person we're with or expose our inner selves too much. A casual scene with a casual partner is typically just a straight technical or mechanical affair, and that's that.

There's nothing wrong with this sort of arrangement. For the sorts of BDSM wants or needs which can be met in a strictly scene-based context—such as a straight need for pain, or for some physiological release through bondage—well-defined and limited scenes can be fine.

UNDERSTANDING BDSM RELATIONSHIPS

What happens between two people who have a long-standing relationship is very different to this.

Firstly, they are prepared to invest in each other. In a long-term relationship of any sort, there is an understanding that not every day or every encounter is going to be perfectly wonderful for both people. Sometimes things aren't going to work due to distractions, medical issues, and other transient problems which affect us all at some time or another. Any scene these people do together doesn't need to be balanced in the sense that each gets their needs met then and there. Instead, they look more at the long term, and if a scene doesn't work out today, maybe it'll work out tomorrow. This is not the case in play with a strictly casual partner where there is only one chance to get it right and where the pressure to perform can be much higher.

Secondly, with people who know each other, there's not so much need to tightly contain the scene or to tightly contain yourself. The scene can afford to run over time. Its effects—such as when you enjoy being tied up so much that you want to stay tied up all night and through until the morning—can even afford to leak into the next day because any time and availability problems can often be flexibly managed. There isn't the same need to pack up and be Joe or Jane Normal straight afterwards as there can be in casual encounters.

And with someone you know you can afford to open up, knowing that your partner is not going to feel burdened by your tears, and that they're not going to be judgemental if you show weaknesses.

Even when your partner isn't a live-in lover, husband, or wife, knowing that they aren't going to disappear from your life means that you don't have to be so independent. You don't have to make sure that a scene and all its psychological and emotional ramifications end when the ropes come off, when the knife is

Foundations of a BDSM relationship

cleaned and put away, or when the floggers are put back in the toy bag. This creates a very different, more open, trusting context in which scenes can play out.

This doesn't mean that there's anything more than topping and bottoming going on between you and your partner, nor does it suggest that there's any 24/7, D&s, or power/control aspect to what you do together.

The important thing is that having a long-standing and ongoing relationship with your play partner does dramatically change the context of your play, as well as create opportunities for play which scratches different sorts of itches than strictly casual play with a casual partner.

Overlap

Being part of a relationship where the relationship itself provides satisfaction (such as M/s or D&s) doesn't prevent you from engaging in more "traditional" BDSM pursuits—such as wax play, bondage, or caning. Indeed, the overarching power/authority relationship can provide a powerful context itself for these other activities.

For example, being compelled by your master to engage in BDSM scenes at his pleasure can be an effective context in which to explore and exercise power. The feeling of having no choice but to obey and submit to the pain or torture he wishes to inflict can be a very intense experience for both you and your master.

6.4 Discussion

An extremely quick way of considering what you're looking for in a BDSM relationship can be summarised as:

- What are you looking for?
- How often do you want it?
- How intense does it need to be?

This takes a lot of the fine detail away from the topic, but these three questions can nevertheless provide a good starting point for determining what's going to work for you.

We can supplement these questions with a further three to give an idea about how a potential partner is going to fit in:

- What are you prepared to give back to your partner?
- How often?
- How much of an effort are you prepared to make?

Consider these carefully. If you're actually just looking for occasional intense BDSM scenes, then a partner who is looking for something more regular or even live-in might be disappointed.

Chapter 7

Compatibility

For a BDSM relationship to work between two people, there has to be some measure of compatibility. We can think of it as being:

- Some or all of the wants and needs you have being satisfied by your partner, by the relationship, or by both, and

- Some or all of the wants and needs your partner has being satisfied by you, by the relationship, or by both.

There are many different wants and needs which might be involved in a BDSM relationship. For example:

- You might want someone to share your interest in shiny nipple clamps,

UNDERSTANDING BDSM RELATIONSHIPS

- You might be looking for a relationship in which to explore long-term, profound submission,
- You might want someone as an occasional bondage-and-sex partner,
- You might be trying to find a partner simply to accompany you to BDSM parties,
- You might be needing someone to tie you up regularly,
- You might be wanting to find a submissive partner with whom to satisfy your need to control or overwhelm,
- You might be looking for a house-mate who shares your passion for wax play, or
- You might be simply looking for cuddles and affection with an occasional hint of BDSM.

Regardless of what your reasons are, you need to make sure that any partner you select has a reasonable chance of satisfying your wants or needs. Sometimes it can be too easy to be distracted by the wrapping—the clothes, the leather, the way of talking, the skills with a flogger, or the knack with a knife. When this sort of distraction occurs, the result can be briefly exciting, but it can also quickly fade. If all you're looking for is a quick bit of excitement—the BDSM equivalent of a one-night stand—then this could be entirely fine. If you're looking for something which will last, you have to pay attention to the real criteria which need to be met for the relationship to work for you in any long-term sense.

At the same time that you're picking a partner for yourself, you need to be sure that you will be able to contribute towards satisfying your potential partner's own wants and needs. This is very important because it's sometimes easy to skip over the fact that your potential BDSM partner also has wants and needs which their relationship with you must satisfy. In the heat of the moment, you might think that you have found Master Magnificent or Subbie Superb and proceed at full speed to attain them without considering or realising that you might not be right for him or her. This can be a difficult thing to accept or admit, but the price you may have to pay for not doing so—namely, ending up in a badly-functioning relationship, or being rejected down the track—is far higher than accepting the inevitable now and devoting your time and energy towards finding a better match.

When you're looking for a BDSM partner, the responsibility for making the relationship work is shared by you both. To make the right—or, at least, the best—choices you need to talk, be honest about your goals, discuss your wants and needs as much as you know about them, and listen to your potential partner as they do the same. Regardless of on which end of the flogger you normally find yourself, you need to learn what works for your potential partner and how to help them get it. While power, control, and authority might lie in the hands of the dominant, that doesn't ever absolve the submissive from making an effort.

Sometimes in the BDSM world you can find the strange ideas that firstly, dominants are the ones who both make relationships work and who have all the responsibility, and secondly, that the submissives are the ones who merely follow. This isn't the case. Each person involved, be they dominant, submissive, top, bottom, master, mistress, or slave, has just as much responsibility as their partner for the success or failure of the relationship. Some submissives think that because they are capable of achieving a deep sub-space, or because they can have multiple orgasms at the drop of a flogger, this must clearly be sufficient for a line of dominants to form at their door with each dominant being desperate to bring the submissive unbridled bliss. This is not so.

7.1 It's doing to, rather than doing with

One of the important differences between a BDSM relationship and a vanilla relationship is that in BDSM you do things *to* your partner while in vanilla relationships you do things *with* your partner. In vanilla relationships or in vanilla sex, it is sufficient merely to do things with someone else. In BDSM it is not.

This difference between doing to and doing with involves the idea of penetration. In a vanilla relationship you might go to a movie together, to dinner together, or out para-sailing together. But, even if the experiences are intense, it isn't your partner causing them. It is the movie, the dinner, or the para-sailing. With BDSM however, we cut our partner with a knife, we tie them up, or we crawl at their feet and beg. In BDSM, we do things directly to our partner. We make them feel. We create the experience. We don't just keep them company while exciting things happen.

This is a big difference in terms of relationships. It means that the BDSM relationships themselves create the opportunities for satisfaction, pleasure, and excitement. We don't merely accompany our partner; we engage them. If I want to see an action movie or have a great dinner then it's easy to find a cinema or a restaurant to satisfy this desire with or without a partner. If I want an intense bondage scene however, I need a strong relationship with someone who is going to be part of that scene with me.

Seeing this difference helps us to understand one of the ways in which a BDSM relationship can fail—namely when the doing to stops happening and all that is left is the doing with. This is the vanilla-fication of a BDSM relationship. Instead of it being about BDSM any more, it somehow fades and you suddenly discover one day that you are living a vanilla relationship.

7.2 Changing needs and personal growth

Sometimes people's BDSM wants and needs change over time. While some needs may vary depending on life's circumstances—such as stressful days possibly leading to a stronger desire for heavy floggings, or that being on holidays may allow time for longer and more relaxed scenes—as people grow and learn about themselves this might change their BDSM wants or needs in longer-term or more profound ways.

Someone who discovers that an aversion for some particular BDSM activity is due to something from their past may work on it and then find that they really enjoy the activity. Someone else may use BDSM as a way of dealing with other issues in their lives, and when they resolve those issues they find that they're no longer interested in BDSM. And some people who never had any interest in BDSM for the first decades of their lives may find themselves drawn to it as they learn more about what makes them tick and as hungers are discovered or recognised.

This is important to understand for a relationship because as time goes by, the wants and needs of the people involved may genuinely change. This change may draw the partners closer together, or it may push them apart. Personal growth doesn't always happen in the direction that is going to strengthen a relationship. It may simply do the opposite.

On the other hand, change itself doesn't mean the end of the relationship. Even if activities you previously enjoyed no longer inspire you, that doesn't mean there aren't other things which can take their place. As your passions for different things wax and wane, talk about the changes with your partner. Don't cover things up and don't pretend to be interested in activities which no longer rock your boat. Keep your partner informed and treat the changes as opportunities to engage in new activities or to see your relationship in new ways.

Chapter 8

Life aspects

A useful way of understanding the place BDSM has in our own relationships is to consider which aspects of our lives we want it to effect or to be involved in.

As I noted earlier, some people make a particular effort to compartmentalise BDSM by confining it to only one or two aspects of their lives. One of the most common ways is by limiting BDSM activities to the bedroom and to sex. Such compartmentalising can be a good way of managing BDSM in the face of conflicting demands on our time and attentions.

For example, when we're talking about a couple with children, limiting BDSM to the bedroom can be a very effective way of keeping BDSM out of the sight of the children. The couple is going to be having sex anyway (probably) and will be making any necessary arrangements to ensure that they can do it in privacy. By satisfying their BDSM wants and needs at the same time, they can kill two birds with one stone.

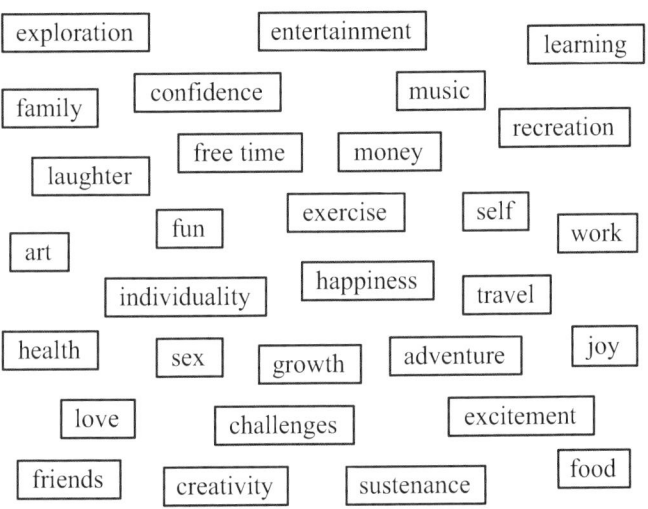

Figure 8.1: Life aspects

UNDERSTANDING BDSM RELATIONSHIPS

While sex is a common companion to BDSM, there are many other aspects of life which can be involved either directly or tangentially with BDSM. I've listed some of these in figure 8.1 on the preceding page to give you a few ideas. It's worth thinking about these and whether they have a place or not in your BDSM now, or whether they could have a place in your BDSM in the future.

Throughout the course of the day there may be opportunities to interact BDSM-wise with others who aren't our primary partners. **Friends** who are either into BDSM themselves, or who are aware of our inclinations, provide chances for us to express our interest in BDSM, to talk about it, or just to try a few things, even when it's not to the extent which we might explore with a primary partner or in a fully-fledged BDSM scene.

Is this something which might actually add to your friendships? Can you meet people through your BDSM social life or at BDSM parties who can become friends away from a party or outside of a dungeon?

Exploration and discovery are aspects of our natural human curiosity. We like to find out new things. In fact, it can be immensely satisfying to speculatively try something and find out that it's the best thing since sliced bread. In BDSM, this can involve new techniques for existing things we do, new sensations, new thoughts, and new feelings. When we are open with our partners, new things become easier to try because we don't feel so awkward about asking, and we don't feel so afraid or worried that something we'd like to explore may turn out to be a dud. Exploring lets us discover new things which we can add to our BDSM repertoire. This adds variety, and gives us more tools to try in different situations. It's worthwhile to take time to try

Life aspects

new things and treat the attempts as little voyages of discovery into uncharted and potentially exciting realms of BDSM.

Entertainment and **fun** are things we might not directly think about as goals for our BDSM. As a top, I might make an extra effort to tie knots with a flourish, or take some time before a flogging to discuss my collection of whips, canes, and floggers with my partner before I get started. It might be that this doesn't add directly to the BDSM component of the activities, or affect my stamina or where I hit, but it changes what we do from a simple flogging scene to something more encompassing and rewarding.

Learning is something for which BDSM provides ample opportunities. The obvious things, such as mechanical technique for impact play, cutting, or bondage, are there for us to learn, but BDSM also gives us a rare chance to see and experience our partners and others we play with at their most vulnerable and helpless. There are many situations and reactions which we get to see that are beyond what we might see in vanilla-land.

Food is not normally mentioned in BDSM handbooks, except possibly when talking about molten chocolate and formal meals served by your slave. But food is an aspect of life which can be touched by BDSM in all sorts of ways. Just as some people can seamlessly combine sex and BDSM, the scene-like nature of eating also lends itself to BDSM-ification. There's no reason, for example, why you can't deny your submissive food for the better part of the day and then tie and torture her with nipple clamps, fruit, floggers, cake, and rope.

Family can be brothers, sisters, mother, father, etc., but for many people into BDSM, particularly those into longer-term D&s or M/s relationships, it can be important to have supportive fellow masters and slaves to lean on and to share with. These can become a sort of family, providing a similar hierarchy with the head of the household and other family members all contributing to the family as a whole.

When you think about **money** and BDSM, maybe what comes to mind is that there's a door charge to your favourite party, or that an upcoming equipment safari for your new dungeon is going to cost big bucks.

Something else you can think about is: can BDSM become part of how you earn your living? Do you have skills or talents which you can put to work? Are you good at handicrafts? Have you thought of making and selling floggers, for example? Well-balanced and well-constructed floggers are keenly sought after because the ones you find in many kinky sex shops are not really intended for serious use by someone who knows what they're doing. Being able to make them, especially if you can make them to order, could be a good side business. Or, if you are good at carpentry you might be able to make and sell St. Andrews crosses, spanking benches, equipment racks, and all sorts of other things. If you're into the social side of things and have the space, have you thought about organising or running play parties for local enthusiasts? Or maybe you could set up a little business supplying some of the more difficult-to-find items which many BDSMers like, such as bondage tape which doesn't stick to the skin, or low-temperature wax-play candles. And, of course, if you like being spanked, you can hire out your backside by the hour, or if you're good with a flogger or with rope, you can tie people up and flog them and get paid for it.

UNDERSTANDING BDSM RELATIONSHIPS

The potential for creativity and art to enter into our BDSM and our BDSM relationships is huge and I have devoted a whole later chapter to it[1].

BDSM often provides opportunities to learn about ourselves. It can be challenging because many of the ideas involved in BDSM can be confronting, but as part of getting involved in BDSM we learn to deal with these things and through this we can gain more self-confidence and a better understanding of who we are.

While all the above have to do with more-or-less direct involvement of BDSM, sometimes the things we learn from BDSM can be useful in other areas of our lives. Learning to take control and be authoritative in a D&s or an M/s context, for example, is a skill which you can transfer and use at the office or with non-BDSM friends. This doesn't mean that you need to be rude, arrogant, or rough, but recognising when it's useful to take charge can be effective and productive and can help keep things moving when people get stuck with making a decision or are in conflict. It can help you be seen as a leader.

Likewise, experience with D&s and M/s can let you recognise when someone you spend time with, such as a colleague or a friend, is inclined to either be dominant or to be submissive. When you see this, and when it works for you, you can allow yourself to respond a little. You don't necessarily need to do a full-scale BDSM conversion on them, but merely let that side of them come out in little ways for your mutual benefit.

If they seem naturally deferential or service-oriented, you can create opportunities for them to express it. Ask them, in a polite way, to get you a coffee, and you may well make their day.

---

[1] Chapter 10 on page 125, *Artists and tinkerers*.

Chapter 9

People

There's one thing which we can be sure about in regards to BDSM, and that is that the physical side of BDSM—the flogging, the bondage, the torture, and the pain—is not it. By *it* I mean the endpoint, the goal, the destination that we BDSM practitioners are trying to attain when we do *what it is that we do*[1].

This may seem like a radical idea when you look at the wide range of popular BDSM books out there which tell us how to focus on and excel at precisely these things. But, the real point of BDSM is not about how many floggers you own or how many ways you can wield them, or how many different types of rope you have in your toy bag and how many different types of knot you can tie, or about the wildly varying selection of candles

---

[1] Sometimes abbreviated as WIITWD.

which you have on hand to create trails of cooling hot wax on flesh. If it were only about the knots, the red marks, and the pain, then I have a clove hitch, a red felt marker, and a house brick which will really make your day.

The actual doing is not why we are into BDSM. It is where the doing takes us psychologically, emotionally, and even spiritually. Indeed, it is actually about people. It is about us. It is not about floggers, ropes, or wax.

BDSM is a complex beast which many people fail to appreciate fully. Many people choose to see BDSM as merely being about kinky sex, which it may well be in part for some, either because that's honestly all that they see or need from it, or because that's all they are prepared to admit they want from it. Frequently it is not quite so easily categorised.

> *This reality, the sadomasochistic reality, kept me going. It was where I explored everything fascinating about human nature, conflict and resolution, passion and control, anger and conditional love. I ignored the nagging voice in me, which I still occasionally call The Chastiser, which continually wondered why the fuck I was doing this, what I was seeking - [ANTONIOU1995].*

9.1 The focus seems to have drifted away from people

It seems that the focus of mainstream BDSM has drifted away from people and is instead moving towards things and the mechanics of things. It can be that dealing with the mechanical side of BDSM—such as how to use a flogger safely, how to tie a person so they can be released quickly in case of blood circulation problems or fainting, how to perform needle play, how to disinfect implements, and so on—is easier than learning what it is that makes you or your partner tick. This mechanical side of BDSM is also much easier to consider than confronting the difficult challenges of navigating a relationship.

Have a look at figure 9.1 on the next page. This is a typical ad for a BDSM workshop. Note that there's no mention of learning how to make it satisfying and rewarding for you and your partner. By the end of the workshop, you may be able to flog in a technically proficient manner. Maybe afterwards you'll be able to throng with the flogging literati, sip fine wine, and discuss the merits of the latest hand-made floggers from the dedicated, if perverted, monks toiling away in quiet solitude in the El Floggo monastery of northern Spain. But will you know how to tell if a flogging is really working for you and your partner and, if not, how to fix it? Will you learn how to recognise what your partner is feeling? Will you know what to say and how to treat your partner? Sorry. These things are not covered.

This is disappointing. How many BDSM folk do you know who have broken up with their partners due to an inadequacy in flogging technique, or through not owning a large enough variety of rope, or due to not being able to discuss corsets or chain *ad infinitum*? Perhaps there are the occasional people for whom a Herculean flogging arm is a requirement for their partner, or who absolutely need their partner to go into the deepest sub-space at the drop of a flogger. Perhaps... though I haven't met any of them yet.

The point I'm trying to make here is that a BDSM-based relationship doesn't collapse because someone has the wrong

> **Flogging 101 by Master FloggingDude**
>
> Due to popular demand we'll be running our Flogging 101 workshop again on the 15th of May. Flogging is one of the most popular BDSM scenes and this workshop will teach you how to get the most out of it.
>
> We'll be looking at:
>
> - The different types of whips and floggers,
> - How to choose a flogger that's right for you,
> - How to prepare a flogging scene, and
> - What to do and what not to do.
>
> Bring a partner if you can because this is a hands-on workshop. If you can't bring a partner we should be able to find someone to work with you. There'll be a number of experienced instructors on-hand and there'll be plenty of time for questions.
>
> What to bring:
>
> - You,
> - A partner, if you have one, and
> - Your own floggers or you can use ours.
>
> 2pm start.

Figure 9.1: Typical BDSM workshop ad

floggers on hand or because their knots are all saggy[2]. People move on because the BDSM itself is not working, not because of knots.

In a sense, I think that BDSM has become a reflection of the take-total-responsibility-for-yourself, fake-empowerment attitude that pervades our western society. You are required to be responsible for your own world and your own experiences. I may flog you or tie you up, but it's entirely up to you to have a good time. If you don't have a good time... well, that's not my fault. It must be you because I did everything right! The workshop mentioned in the ad above is an ideal example of this. The focus isn't on getting a satisfying or powerful experience. It's about the technical execution of floggings, just add submissive!

Perhaps this drift towards the mechanical is also due to a wider trend towards political correctness.

> *Now it's three-hundred-page manuals on how to make sure nothing bad will ever happen to you and twelve-page party rules that state that the utmost care must be taken to make sure that no one is frightened or offended, that no bodily fluids are spilled, and no cries shock the neighbors - [ANTONIOU1995].*

Being politically correct seems to mean that you don't impact on the lives of other people and that you keep your distance. Good and effective BDSM is contrary to this. It's about engaging and penetrating your partner. It's about having an effect on them. It's about doing *to* them.

---

[2]Like mine.

Understanding BDSM Relationships

If you do decide to start treading in the areas where you actually have a real impact on your partner's psychological, emotional, or spiritual experience, then you are taking on a whole lot more responsibility and power than if you're just saying, "Here! Let me flog you." Indeed, perhaps it is fear of this power and responsibility which causes so many people to focus on the "safe" mechanical side of BDSM.

BDSM is fundamentally about people, not about things, implements, or dungeons. When a BDSM relationship fails it's not because the floggers weren't right or because the dungeon was under-equipped. It's because of a people failure. BDSM is about how people feel. It's about their wants and needs. And mostly it's about their relationships with other people. Sometimes—perhaps too often—we forget this.

When a BDSM relationship succeeds, when it flowers, when it meets the deepest needs of the two people involved, it doesn't do so because of dungeon furniture, because of coils of rope, or because of shiny nipple clamps. It succeeds because of the people. It's easy for this people aspect of BDSM to slip our minds. Shiny new nipple clamps, the smell of leather from our floggers, a bright array of multi-coloured candles, the sting of the whip, and the texture of the rope can all distract us.

When things get difficult it can be oh-so-tempting to focus on the mechanical side of it all: on how to flog, on how to disinfect, on how to tie knots, on how to clean our kit when we're done, on how to quickly slip a hypodermic needle tip through a fold of skin, and so on.

While being able to tie knots might be an excellent talent to have, unless there are people skills behind the knots then they will merely be knots and not the path to ecstasy, self enlightenment, or even a good fuck. Without the ability to interact, to explore, to understand, to share, and to experience BDSM with your partner, the BDSM itself can and will be hollow.

What I'm talking about here are two of the themes of this book: penetration and engagement. The mechanical aspects of BDSM—the knots, the floggers, the dungeons, and so on—are tools which we use to engage and penetrate our partners. They aren't the endpoint by any means. We don't go to workshops about bondage or electroplay just so we're technically proficient. Technical proficiency might be nice, but we go to these workshops to learns skills which we can use to engage and penetrate our partners.

In short, we could say that the goal of all this engagement and penetration is to create or to increase *happiness*. We don't just stick hypodermic needles into our partners because we want to increase their metal content or because we want to make them magnetic, and we don't encourage our partners to tie us up because we think they only like to see us immobile, and we don't stand at one end or the other of a whip because pain is the end station. There has to be some positive outcome beyond the activity itself for what we do. That's why we do it. It might be something simple like a quick case of the jollies, a bit of a laugh, maybe an orgasm; or it could be something more profound, such as deep surrender, an opportunity to learn something about ourselves or our partners, or an intimate bonding experience.

Something we don't always notice is that a BDSM relationship can provide an opportunity to be more of ourselves than other circumstances allow. Having a trusted and receptive partner allows you to show more parts of yourself and to say and do more things than you might be able to with someone else. We aren't simply intellectual creatures who show ourselves through carefully chosen words and the occasional gesture. We are

People

animals who can and do need to communicate through actions, aggression, sex, dominance, and submission. Being able to use rope to "speak", or to use a heavy flogger to send a very primal message, or to kneel and make ourselves helpless and vulnerable to our partner, are all ways to communicate with our partner at a level other than words. Being able to do this can be a very deep form of penetration and can effect us profoundly. It can be giving life and voice to parts of ourselves which we must normally keep quiet, and can let those parts of ourselves be active and fulfil themselves. This self expression is a form of release. We can look at it as BDSM providing a way of letting ourselves be or become.

In the rest of this chapter I'd like to expand on a few of the things I've just been talking about, and I'd like to look at a few of the other things which BDSM can mean for us and our partners.

9.2 Activities

The focus of this book is people—people mainly in the form of our partners, but also in the form of anyone with whom we establish any sort of relationship for the purpose of exploring or meeting wants and needs through BDSM. The penetration part of this occurs through what we do with these people, through what we do with our partners.

When we talk about BDSM activities, we often see them in terms of what is done to submissives. Outwardly, submissives seem to be the ones who are being penetrated by flogging, bondage, mummification, piercing, and so on. The poor little dominants toiling away in the background might hardly get a mention. However, being on the other end of the flogger, rope, cling wrap,

Understanding BDSM Relationships

or needle can be just as exciting and satisfying. That is why dominants do it. To use a sexual analogy: being the one with the dick doesn't make sex any less exciting or pleasurable for a man because he is the one doing the penetrating rather than being the one who is penetrated. My point is that we BDSM folk tend to define what we do in relation to what happens to the submissives, even though the outcome for a dominant can be just as satisfying or profound—such as catharsis, surrender, sexual arousal, or even service.

Generally speaking, if we aren't there with them, or we have no contact with them, then we can't penetrate our partners. It is through the activities we actually do with our partners, or through the consequences of these activities, that we penetrate them and they penetrate us. Or, put another way, we make manifest penetration and engagement through the activities we explore with our partners. Without activities there is no penetration and, consequently, there is no engagement.

In what follows, I want to talk about a number of the activities we do in BDSM with a focus on the relationship side of them. How can and do they effect a relationship? How do they help us penetrate or be penetrated by our partners? How can we engage our partners more when we do them?

Terminology

Labels such as bottom, submissive, or slave get used a lot in BDSM. Often, these terms aren't terribly useful because: a) there are only seven terms[3] and they're hardly enough to describe

---

[3] Master, mistress, dominant, submissive, top, bottom, and switch.

People

the very large variety of attitudes, practices, wants, needs, and desires which we find in BDSM, and b) there's no common agreement on what these terms mean. Even if we could nail down what our regular BDSM companions intend by these terms, we can easily come across other people who use these terms very differently.

The same labelling problem which occurs for bottoms, submissives, and slaves occurs for tops, dominants, mistresses, and masters. The terms are blurred by inconsistent use. The terms "master" and "mistress" are particularly abused and there's a common convention of calling anyone on the handle-end of a flogger or anyone who ties knots, regardless of how well or not, "master" or "mistress" even though by some definitions they might more accurately be described as simply a top.

This is compounded by the fact that there are actually folk around who we can correctly call "masters" because they are master artisans. They are genuine experts at their craft—be it at wielding a cane, making bondage furniture, tying knots, crafting a perfectly-balanced flogger, or whatever.

For some people too, there's a sort of implicit expectation that a master or mistress is someone who masters slaves, who commands authority and obedience, and whose personal aura overwhelms all of those who come before them. Not all masters and mistresses do this. Some masters and mistresses simply top, often dedicating themselves to it and doing it very well.

Until there's some central BDSM labelling authority, linguistic purists such as myself are just going to have to put up with this uncomfortable blurring of terms. For the rest of this chapter I am however going to make my writing life, and your reading life, easier. I am simply going to group tops, dominants, mistresses and masters together and refer to them as "dominants", and I'm going to group bottoms, slaves, and submissives together and refer to them as "submissives".

Pain

Many submissives look for pain. Sometimes people talk about this as a type of masochism, but in reality submissives want or need pain which they can use to get somewhere emotionally or psychologically. The pain itself is not pleasurable or rewarding, but where it takes the submissive is.

The physical pain a submissive looks for tends to be quite localised, usually limited to a small part of the body such as the buttocks, the shoulders, nipples, etc. More wide ranging pain, such as along the length of both legs, is generally simply painful and isn't useful.

Most commonly in the BDSM world, pain comes from impact play—being hit by a cane, a flogger, a whip, or by being spanked. There are a couple of reasons why this sort of pain is the most common. One of the main ones is that it's easily controllable. The submissive's partner can vary how hard they hit and the rate at which they hit to create just the right level of pain. There are also a wide variety of implements which can be used and these allow the pain to be *tuned* to exactly what the submissive needs.

A second reason why impact play is a common source of pain is that it involves the submissive's partner. Indeed, impact play done on oneself is very rarely satisfying. By having a partner do the striking it means that both partners are intimately involved in this powerful experience. The submissive can also surrender themselves more and immerse themselves more in the experience because their partner takes care of the mechanical aspects.

There are other sources of pain and although they're quite common, they aren't generally as popular as impact play.

Using clamps or alligator clips on sensitive body parts—particularly nipples, labia, lips, and testicles—is easy, relatively safe for short periods, and the intensity of the pain can be varied by adjusting the tightness of the clamps.

Cutting, the use of a sterile knife to cut through outer layers of skin, is another source of frequently intense pain.

There can be many effects of pain. A submissive might see pain as something to resist or overcome. It might be a test of strength, not against their partner, but against the pain itself. Or they may see it as something which drives everything else out of their mind and leaves them feeling empty and cleansed. It can also be a release. If the pain isn't sharp, such as the thudding from some types of flogger, it might take them into a unique and intensely focused state of mind (sub-space). Where the pain is targeted between their legs, they may find it an intense amplification of sexual penetration. And finally, pain might be a tool which leads the submissive into a state of complete surrender, and this can be a deep and spiritual experience.

When the pain is a tool the submissive uses to reach some psychological, emotional, or spiritual destination it's important to appreciate that too little pain, too much pain, or the wrong sort of pain can make it hard or even impossible for the submissive to get where they want to go. This is where their dominant plays an important role. It is rarely the case that a submissive just needs one sort of pain. Usually, they need a progression of different types of pain, or of different ways the pain is applied, or of different rhythms of pain as they move through different states of mind. Explaining this to their dominant as it happens would be distracting and so the ability of their dominant to determine on their own what pain is required, when to change the pace, when to pause, etc., can be vital for a submissive.

Previous experience with other submissives might help a dominant get this right, but when the dominant knows their submissive intimately, knows what they need, and knows how to read the signals their submissive sends throughout the scene—such as muscle contractions, how the submissive changes position, and so on—then the dominant is going to know what to do and when to do it. Of course, I'm talking about one of my themes in this book: engagement. The road paved with pain which the submissive travels is going to be smoother and with less detours when their dominant engages them personally, rather than engages only An Average Submissive.

When the pain isn't quite right, or is merely adequate, a submissive has to work harder to adapt what they're getting from their dominant to achieve what they need, and this can make the experience or scene less immersive.

Bondage

Bondage is another common BDSM activity. Although it doesn't hurt, it has many things in common with the sorts of pain we see elsewhere in BDSM. Firstly, it's controllable—a skilled bondage artist can tie or untie someone very quickly and the degree of restraint can vary from simple rope handcuffs to full mummification. Secondly, although there are a few people who practice self-bondage, bondage is most effective when done by a partner. Bondage can create powerful feelings of helplessness and of being controlled. It's also a tool for objectification in a couple of ways.

Understanding BDSM Relationships

Firstly, the general physiological definition for a human includes: one head, two arms, two legs, and a torso. Bondage and mummification reduce this. The arms might still be there, but when they're tied a submissive is rendered arm-less, becoming less than before. The same thing can happen when their legs are tied, or when a mask is put on, or when a gag is inserted in their mouth. As well as compelling the submissive to a state of surrender or submission, all of these things reduce the submissive to being less of a person. They take away part of their humanity. They begin to objectify them.

Secondly, depending on how they're tied, a submissive becomes useful to a dominant in ways which they are not when they're not tied. If the submissive is hog-tied, or if they're tied to a piece of furniture, they may simply become a hole to fuck. Not a person to fuck, or a submissive to fuck, but a hole that's ready to be used at the dominant's convenience.

And if we're talking about decorative bondage, the submissive becomes simply a canvas on which the knots, rope, and colours are aesthetically arranged.

With the large variety of ways bondage can be applied—and we haven't even talked about cages, chains, bondage furniture, suspension bondage, or outdoor bondage—it's obvious that there are lots of opportunities for engagement. Basic ties, such as rope handcuffs or hog-ties, tend to be effective for most submissives, but we're trying to talk about actual submissives rather than Average Submissives in this book and when you have a regular partner you can explore things which are particular for you both. For example, outdoor bondage, particularly while naked, is very effective for some, but not all, submissives. Suspension bondage can be exciting and a real challenge for both the dominant and the submissive, but it's not everyone's cup of tea. The important thing is that with such a variety of options, when bondage is something that works for you and your partner it provides a large field for you both to intimately explore and may contain some hidden treasures.

Finally, the tight embrace of rope can create a physiological response in some people, simply giving them satisfying or pleasant feelings of floating, detachment, or release[4].

Foreplay for sex

Pain play, impact play, and bondage are common precursors to sex. For some people they can act as a sort of foreplay, even while being satisfying for other wants and needs at the same time. They can leave a submissive feeling powerfully penetrated, and can leave a dominant feeling that he has powerfully penetrated his partner. As a result of the play, the dominant and the submissive can become highly aroused and ready for some sexual action.

On the other hand, some forms of BDSM play can be draining and not leave any energy for sex. An intense cutting scene, where designs are cut into the submissive's flesh by their dominant partner, might not leave the submissive feeling horny at all. A heavy interrogation scene, or some humiliation play, might leave the submissive feeling cleansed and refreshed, but not necessarily ready for some between-the-sheets action. Instead, they might just want some quiet time to recover.

---

[4][GRANDIN1992] and [KRAUSS1987].

When a submissive or dominant is looking to use BDSM as foreplay for sex, there are a few activities which can be very effective:

- Sensation play - using touch, heat, cold, feathers, sandpaper, and so on, to create various sensations, often when the submissive is bound or blindfolded,

- Wax or candle play - the dripping of hot, molten wax onto the submissive—such as on their breasts or back—and letting it cool and set on their skin,

- Sensual flogging - using soft floggers to gently strike the skin of a submissive, perhaps near or on their genitals and breasts, or

- Light bondage - using ropes, silk scarves, or handcuffs to render a submissive helpless to the sexual advances of their dominant partner.

Notable about all of these is that they're not intense or draining, and they involve a lot of physical contact which is potentially quite arousing.

Humiliation

Humiliation play actually has something in common with bondage. Where bondage subtracts from someone physically by taking away their power to move parts of their body, humiliation attempts to remove parts of their identity, their self, their pride, or their self-respect. By criticising someone or by mocking them when they cannot defend themselves, humiliation diminishes them. Like bondage, this diminution is under the dominant's control. The dominant chooses what to say or what to compel the submissive to do, and the dominant acquires the control and power to re-value the submissive, to make them either feel less of a person or more of a person as the dominant chooses.

This is powerful stuff because it reaches beyond the physical, which most of us are comfortable with, and into the self, which most of us are less comfortable with. We're less comfortable because we often have less skills for dealing with these sorts of deliberate attempts to limit us and thus feel humiliation more strongly than, say, rope bondage.

Other forms of humiliation include being compelled to be naked in front of others, being required to use kitty litter in the corner of the room where we can be watched rather than use a toilet in privacy, and needing to perform something we're not very good at where others can see us.

Engagement has its place here too because not every submissive is going to find the same things humiliating. Just undressing someone, pointing at their private parts and laughing is not going to work for everyone. In fact, humiliation is a risky business. Untying someone and packing the ropes away is easy, but putting someone's self back together, or your relationship, after you've said the wrong thing is not. Knowing your partner intimately and having a history of experience together teaches you what works and what doesn't.

Surrender

One of the most powerful BDSM experiences is surrender, and it is an unspoken, yet very important part of most BDSM activities. Creating pain, restraint, humiliation, or anything else in BDSM is most effective when we can let our defences down and allow these feelings in. In other words, we get most bang for our buck when we can allow ourselves be fully penetrated.

For a submissive to be able to surrender so that this can happen, they need to feel safe, they need to trust that their partner is going to be capable and skilled, and they need to not have any worries or concerns which prevent them from losing themselves in whatever it is that they're doing. Any of these things can get in the way of the process which allows pain or bondage to become pleasure.

Importantly, surrender is just as much a vital part of the experience for submissives as it is for tops, dominants, and masters. A submissive may respond to and be penetrated by what their dominant does to them and by their own reactions to this, while a dominant is penetrated by what they themselves do and by how their submissive partner responds. Surrender is a necessary part of this penetration, and if a dominant doesn't let their own barriers down to allow the experience and their partner to enter them, then no penetration will happen and the dominant will find the experience quite empty.

Punishment or discipline

Another thing which some submissives look for is punishment or discipline. Being put in a position where they endure a clinical, even detached, caning, whipping, or spanking can be emotionally cleansing. It can be a way of releasing pent-up feelings, frustration, or even guilt.

Instead of wanting the experience to be sensual, such as when BDSM is used as sexual foreplay, or instead of wanting it to be a form of pain which they can use to take them into sub-space, these submissives typically look for sharp and genuinely painful pain.

A common scenario which helps to set the psychological scene for discipline can be a schoolgirl or schoolboy being disciplined by a teacher. This is a form of role play which creates the right mood. A school uniform helps, as does the submissive being required to drop their pants or panties and bend over a desk.

Additionally, striking implements more typical of a disciplinary environment, such as a wooden ruler or a short cane, often work best for this. Over-the-knee spankings can also be effective.

Engagement has an important role in punishment. While there are many BDSM activities which are typically associated with the idea of punishment—such as caning, being compelled to stand in the corner (humiliation), or spanking—it's often a very personal thing. Caning involving a custom-made, leather-padded bench in the dungeon might be the stuff of serious red marks and not being able to sit down without wincing for a week, but caning while leaning over an old school desk might be psychologically more profound. Over-the-knee spanking can be pleasurable and give you a radiant butt for hours afterwards, but for some the better effect might involve dropping your pants, leaning over an old-style school desk and receiving six of the best.

Service

Service is attending to the wants and needs of your dominant partner. Well, usually that's what it looks like. In reality, a lot of the time what we're talking about is penetration. The acts of service need to penetrate the submissive. They need to feel that they are serving or being useful. The dominant also needs to be penetrated. He needs to feel the service of his submissive. If you happened to be a dominant and you happened to have a slave who professed that they'd do anything you asked, you could send them to a coal mine to dig coal for you. In BDSM-land this is probably not going to be satisfying for either of you, though you might get some lumps of coal out of it. It's not going to be satisfying relationship-wise because although having coal dug for you might be your greatest wish, you don't get it as part of your relationship with your enthusiastic, and now grubby, submissive. The service is distant from you. It is detached. Your submissive also doesn't experience any penetration by you because your reaction is something she simply doesn't see in the glow of her headlamp down in the mine.

Because we're talking about BDSM here, and because we're particularly talking about BDSM relationships, penetration and engagement need to be present. Service, at least in BDSM, provides a context in which penetration can occur. However, service can become hollow if service is all there is. It might be fine for a real-life butler (or miner), but they get paid for it. Submissives and dominants need penetration as their reward and, again, I'm not necessarily talking about sexual penetration.

For submissives, it might be that they genuinely need to feel that they are taking care of their partner. This is sometimes the case, particularly for female submissives. When so, the service needs to be personal, such as preparing and serving food, helping their partner dress, or personally delivering lumps of coal and putting them in the fireplace. The submissive can see and feel the benefit, and can feel their own need being met as they serve. It often requires the dominant to show that they are pleased and, notably, it is a case where the submissive does the action and the dominant responds, although it is the dominant whose needs are the ultimate driver for the service.

How satisfying, rewarding, or penetrating it is for a submissive to perform service is going to vary greatly. Some submissives might serve to experience the long-term surrender of themselves to the authority of their dominant and it might not actually have anything to do with personal service for them *per se*.

Because service is a case of horses for courses, when you're considering it you don't need to just think about the general idea of service, but you need to consider the type of service. Here are some to consider:

- Being a chauffer,
- Running errands, doing shopping,
- Household duties - such as cleaning, ironing, or cooking,
- Personal service - being a valet,
- Sexual service - being sexually on-call,
- Personal assistant - organising your dominant's appointments, paying bills,
- Being the home handyman - doing repairs around the house or apartment, painting,
- Technical work - maintaining your dominant's web site, and
- Mining coal.

Physical handling

Physical handling is where the dominant uses main force or physical strength to manipulate and control their submissive. For a submissive this can be quite a powerful experience. Being controlled is a common BDSM and sexual drive[5], and actual physical manhandling is a very primal expression of this.

Sometimes physical handling can be quite subtle, such as when a submissive is being tied up by their dominant. During ties, the dominant is often in physical contact with their submissive with incidental touches—such as when they brush against their submissive's skin as they position the rope or knots, or more directly as they place their submissive's arms, legs, head, and body in particular positions as they tie the rope.

More direct physical handling can be in the form of the dominant pushing their submissive to their knees, grabbing them by the hair and dragging them around, or even roughly undressing them and fucking them.

Clearly, there's an element of objectification to this because physical handling moves us away from the hands-off, civilised culture we normally live in and instead moves us towards the animalistic, making us handlers of meat, or making us the meat itself.

To be commanded

Being commanded by a dominant or master can be very powerful and very symbolic for a submissive. I'm not talking about the

---

[5][HILL1996], [MESTON2007].

casual, drive-by commands a dominant might give while they're actually busy with something else. Some submissives' boats are rocked in this regard when commands are given in a serious, or even sanctified context. No jeans and T-shirts here for the dominant. Instead, he or she dresses in their finest and blackest leathers, grasps their submissive firmly by the chin, angles their submissive's head up, fixes the submissive in the eye, adopts a stern, deeper-than-usual, and compelling voice, and then lays down the law.

There may be some fantasy to this, but the goal is for the submissive to feel themselves commanded, to feel the intensity of their partner, and to have their partner's wishes to focus on.

We need to distinguish between being commanded on one hand, and obeying commands on the other because there's not always a one-to-one connection. Many submissives find the experience of interacting with their dominant or master to be the exciting part of their relationship. Being commanded is a very serious and immediate interaction. It is potentially very profound. Actually obeying the commands is not necessarily such a high point though. There are some submissives who revel in being directed or commanded by their partner, but whose interest and obedience rapidly diminishes once the interaction ends... such as when they need to go away and do as they've been told.

This can be a confusing thing for a dominant or master when it first happens, but the key thing to keep in mind is that some submissives require that component of interaction. That is the form of penetration to which they mainly respond. They need to have an immediate sense of the presence of their dominant and to be aware of and feel what their dominant is doing, preferably to them, at all times. Otherwise, their focus wanders to other things which may seem more interesting and penetrating.

People

Perhaps this type of submissive is going to be more suited to BDSM activities and scenes which closely involve their partner—such as dungeon scenes—rather than D&s. Again, we're talking about engagement here. We're talking about knowing your partner and knowing what they respond to.

A submissive may well claim to be intensely service-oriented, but the nature of the service, and the context in which they perform well, can vary dramatically. Only by both talking with and exploring a submissive can you find out the details.

Micromanagement

Rather than simply give a submissive or slave an order or instruction and leave them to work out the details themselves, micromanagement is where a dominant takes a close and active interest in the execution of the order, oversees every particular, and directs or commands his submissive in fine detail as they carry out the order.

When used in the wider or vanilla community, micromanagement has a negative connotation in that it suggests that the person doing the micromanagement is neglecting bigger issues and is making choices and decisions which their minion is perfectly capable of doing on their own. In the BDSM world however, micromanagement can be an exercise of detailed interaction, domination, and surrender. The submissive might be completely capable of cleaning the kitchen or dressing herself on her own, but micromanagement requires that she give up this autonomy and make herself available, almost puppet-like, to her partner as he directs her through these activities.

Like some other activities in BDSM, there can be an element of objectification in micromanagement. Through having her ability to choose how to perform ordinary tasks taken away, her status as a person is reduced and she becomes more and more a puppet whose strings are controlled by her dominant.

In the wider community, micromanagement is often a sign of lack of trust, but in BDSM it can be an effective exercise in control and penetration, requiring close interaction and supervision on the part of the dominant, and this close interaction itself can be the payoff.

This payoff isn't just for the submissive. If we continue with the puppet analogy for a moment, the dominant also gets to feel his submissive partner in the same way a puppeteer feels the weight and resistance of his puppet as he pulls the strings. If there's some unexpected resistance he can pull harder or change the direction he pulls. With his submissive, the dominant can adapt his commands depending on her skills and ability to execute them, and depending on any resistance she displays.

Penetration of a dominant

Following on from what I said earlier, a lot of literature, and even a fair chunk of my own, focuses on the reactions, feelings, needs, and wants of submissives. Often this is the case because a submissive is, in some ways, more *visible* than a dominant. What a submissive suffers and experiences is usually more apparent and more easily viewed than the experiences of a dominant. Submissives are often also louder. However, a dominant also explores BDSM and engages in BDSM activities because they want something out of it, i.e., because they have wants or needs they wish to satisfy through individual BDSM activities or through their BDSM relationships. And, in fact, the same three pillars of BDSM which I mentioned early in this book have the same place in satisfying a dominant as they do in satisfying a submissive.

For example, it must be the case that a dominant experiences penetration. If they aren't affected by their partner or by what they do with their partner then the experience is simply hollow and unfulfilling. And to actually have a BDSM relationship they need to be engaged by their partner. Their partner needs to know them and treat them as the individual they are, rather than just as Another Dominant.

In many cases, the penetration a dominant experiences comes from two sources:

- The first source of penetration is the dominant's own actions. For some dominant's the presence of their submissive can be a chance to let the dominant part of themselves out, to express that part of themselves which they might otherwise need to keep bottled up. For example, a dominant who has a primal need to manhandle or to physically express control or power is going to have that chance to unleash this side of themselves when they're with their willing and receptive partner. Just on its own, this can be a powerful experience, one which the dominant feels deeply inside themselves.

  This self expression doesn't need to be a deep primal urge though. Some dominants might have a creative or artistic side[6] and this part of themselves is something which they can release with their partner. While this sort of activity might not seem as intense as giving a partner a heavy

---
[6] See chapter 10, *Artists and tinkerers*.

beating, it can be just as important and significant to the dominant.

- The second source of penetration is the response of the dominant's partner. Seeing your partner being turned on by what you do, seeing reactions being triggered, or seeing needs being manifested and met, can also have a very strong effect on a dominant. Mother Nature is partly responsible for this by making sure that when we become aroused—and not just sexually—we transmit signals to our partners which trigger them into doing more and becoming more aroused themselves. This happens even when we're not aware that we're sending these signals.

When the little BDSM centre in my brain turns on and I feel like tying someone up or torturing them, this initial stirring may be what actually starts me doing BDSM stuff or what starts me having BDSM thoughts, but the pleasure and satisfaction doesn't just come from actually carrying out these desires. It comes from the reactions of my partner. As they respond and are aroused by what I do, their actions and reactions penetrate and trigger me. As I respond to them and the dynamic we create together, I become more aroused and what I do intensifies, which triggers them to greater heights, which triggers me, and so on. It is an ever-increasing spiral as we penetrate, feed off, and engage each other.

Surrender of a dominant

Surrender is a term we might normally associate with a slave or submissive, but as I noted above, surrender is vital for a dominant as well. In his case, the surrender is of himself to the experience. The dominant must be open to the effect of his own actions, and to the effect on him of the actions and reactions of his partner.

It can be tempting for a dominant to try to be in control all the time and perhaps there is a bit of a misconception about this. Trying to be in control all the time can actually be counterproductive. For example, if you have a skilled and talented service-oriented submissive you can be fully in charge but *delegate* to him or her the tasks you want them to do. You might say to this talented possession of yours, "Make me a fine meal of lasagna with a rich, minced beef filling and a tasty cheese sauce[7]." They can go off on their own and devote themselves to satisfying this desire, and later serve this culinary delight to you. You then surrender to this experience they have prepared for you and soak up any associated wine or dessert. Through all of this—from the initial order to the final burp—you are in charge, but you're not micromanaging. You're delegating and reaping the rewards of the exercise of your authority.

The same upwards spiral of penetration I mentioned above is at play in this situation as well. You don't send your submissive out of the room when you eat. Instead, you might have them dress for the occasion and then keep you company. They are going to see and experience the pleasure they have brought you. And perhaps this will bring out more of the submissive in them as they serve the meal, pour the wine, etc., which might trigger more of Little Dom inside you, and so on.

If you have trouble delegating then it's much harder for your submissive to both contribute to your experience and to create

---

[7] Any female submissives or slaves who want to know how to show me a good time, take note [PM].

situations which penetrate you. Indeed, when you don't let them take their own initiative, they probably can't do much for you at all. Continuing with the lasagne example, if you keep a supervisory eye on every single step of its production then effectively you are cooking it yourself and are just using your submissive as a replacement set of hands for your own. There's no surrender in this for you. If instead you give your partner the initial instruction to make lasagne and then leave them to it, the result is surrender on your part, as well as seeing the results of their determination to serve you well—both of which can be quite penetrating. Micromanaging is a good tool at times, but it can also create a barrier between you and your submissive. And one way to get past that barrier is to surrender yourself to your submissive.

Training

A common activity in a BDSM relationship is training. Exactly what this means can vary from partnership to partnership. For some people it is closely associated with heavy physical play, such as whipping or flogging, and involves habituating the submissive so that he or she is able to endure heavier and longer sessions. The benefit for the dominant is that they don't just finish their own warm-up and find their partner has already reached their pain or tolerance limit. Part of the training in this case might be simply developing endurance, but can also be teaching the submissive ways that their endurance can be prolonged—such as by controlling or pacing their breathing, changing position or flexing their muscles, by performing relaxation exercises, etc.

For other folk, training can be the process by which a dominant teaches a submissive the behaviours and attitudes he wishes them to exhibit as part of their involvement with him. These might be rituals and structured rules[8] which give the submissive an overarching way of behaving outside of direct interactions with their dominant. In addition there will be training in how the dominant wants his submissive to behave in direct interactions, such as when she is giving personal service, when she is receiving orders, when she is speaking, and so on.

In all cases though, the result of training is that the dominant can see and experience the changes he is causing in his partner's behaviour (which is, of course, penetrating her as well).

Empowering

> *Two are better than one; because they have a good reward for their labour. For if they fall, the one will lift up his fellow: but woe to him that is alone when he falleth; for he hath not another to help him up - Ecclesiastes 4:9-10*
>
> *Two heads are better than one - Proverb*

My point with the above two quotations is that when you are a dominant working with your submissive then the two of you together are potentially better than you just working on your own. And because you're the dominant, you are the one in the driver's seat and you get to decide the projects which you both work towards. Instead of it just being you, your submissive can become an extension of you, an extra set of arms, or an extra brain, working towards the goal you set. This can be very

---

[8] See also [MASTERS2009, pp. 143 - 156].

empowering. It can be an intense feeling of being able to do more, of being stronger, of being more potent.

Not only is your submissive partner a fully-functional human being, they are there to be pressed to your will, to enable you to achieve what you want with twice the capability of just you on your own.

Beyond this is something I mentioned earlier, which is allowing you to be yourself, allowing you to express the feelings, desires, lusts, and needs which you can't express with anyone else. Your partner is your target for manhandling and rough treatment. Metaphorically, she is the one you overpower with a club and drag off to your cave. She can also be the one who suffers under your rigorous training regime, or she is the one you role play with, or she is the one you tie with your diabolical array of knots. Your submissive empowers you to be you. And, at the same time, you empower her to be her.

Meditation

For both the dominant and the submissive, many BDSM activities allow them to enter into a reflective mental state somewhat like meditation. This can be a state of intense inwards focus. It's often associated with physical relaxation and sometimes with feelings of floating.

Primitive and not-so-primitive folk sometimes use heavy, regular drumming to get into such a state. Others might use some experience which requires or demands quiet and close attention to some activity. We can easily find such situations in BDSM through things like heavy flogging in the first instance, or through piercing in the second.

People

There can be a strong element of surrender in these sorts of meditative states, and it can often be the case that both the dominant and the submissive react the same way to what's going on.

For example, in a heavy and regular flogging, both dominant and submissive share the same regular thudding, even though they are at opposite ends of the flogger. Similarly, a submissive being pierced with hypodermic needle tips is going to be just as intensely focussed on the placing of each needle as their dominant is in ensuring the needle goes in just right.

This same close attention to what's going on to the exclusion of what's happening around you can occur with some forms of detailed bondage, stylised impact play such as florentine flogging, wax play, and many others.

Catharsis

Catharsis, which I mentioned earlier, is associated with intense or dramatic experiences. It is an outlet for strong, built-up emotions and feelings which can't find an easy release any other way. BDSM has the possibility of this intensity through activities like pain play, heavy flogging or whipping, role play, and others. In contrast to meditation, which is a surrender to what's happening, catharsis can often involve reacting to or against what's happening. For example, a submissive who is tied to an A-frame, who is being heavily flogged, and who is strongly writhing and straining against her bonds, can get a very powerful release through her own physical actions and reactions. This is very different to a quiet meditative state. Similarly, intense role play, such as an interrogation scene, provides many opportunities for drama and emotional release.

In terms of relationships, catharsis has more of a chance of occurring when there is no distraction from the experiences and when limits are well known. When both the dominant and the submissive know themselves and each other well, each can work towards their own catharsis without having to wonder or question what they need to do for their partner because they already know.

Flogging is one BDSM activity which very strongly involves the dominant in the drama. While the outward purpose of a flogging might be to give the submissive a severe hammering, by carefully choosing their floggers and the way they apply them, the dominant can control how much of themselves and their raw effort they put in. Choosing a flogger which requires little effort to wield can distance the dominant from what's happening, while a perhaps shorter or softer flogger can mean that the dominant needs to put more of themselves into getting the same result from their submissive. This extra effort involves the dominant more and gives them potentially more cathartic release.

9.3 Conclusion

When we look at BDSM—both at the activities we do and then at the relationships we have with our BDSM partners—we can find that although the activities themselves can be rewarding and satisfying in themselves, the relationship we have with our partner changes the nature of our activities and the effect they have on us.

Trust is a big part of this, and it is a major contributor to how much we can surrender. This directly impacts how profound our experiences are.

Understanding BDSM Relationships

In addition, when we explore BDSM in the context of a longer-term relationship we have the option of allowing our activities to become less scene-based and to embed aspects of our activities in what we do outside of the dungeon. For example, if we talk about a couple who like rope, the dominant can tie his partner into a rope harness at the beginning of the day and let her go to work wearing it under her clothes. This can create a low-level penetration for both of them for a whole day. Or, when we talk about D&s, a dominant can decide in the morning what his submissive will be eating and drinking during lunch or during any breaks she has while working.

Longer-term relationships also create the opportunity to learn our partner's particular interests, preferences, and triggers so that what we do engages them and is targeted at them and their needs. This increases the satisfaction we both get. A possible analogy is off-the-shelf clothing versus tailored clothing. It can take a long time to go through a rack of clothing looking for something which is the right fit, and there's no guarantee that you'll actually find what you need anyway. Tailor-made clothing, clothing made exactly for you, will be the right fit every time. When we as dominants or submissives know our partner's BDSM "measurements", then what we do can be a perfect fit for them most, if not all, the time.

What we do in BDSM creates opportunities to engage our partners, not just to do technical proficient BDSM scenes. This engagement, finding and recognising our partner as an individual instead of just as A Submissive or A Dominant, is what makes a BDSM relationship.

Chapter 10

Artists and tinkerers

BDSM frequently provides opportunities to be creative. Sometimes these opportunities can be quite obvious. Shibari, a style of bondage focussing on the visual appearance of the bound figure and on the pattern of the ropes and knots, is a good example.

There are many other ways for creativity to appear in a BDSM context. Recognising that this is happening is important in terms of a relationship because it may be that a creative or artistic outlet is very significant either to you, or to your partner, or to you both. When it is, it needs to be supported and encouraged just as any other want or need. If it isn't recognised and supported, it's like you spending a week or more painting a fine erotic mural on your bedroom walls and then finding that your partner complains that it doesn't match the pillow cases. You end up feeling that the effort which you've put in to enrich your life and theirs with art has suddenly been treated as valueless.

In the context of actual BDSM activities, creativity can show up in a number of ways. Beyond Shibari (and erotic wall murals) there are also:

- Patterns of lines created on someone's butt from caning,
- Patterns of needles placed during piercing, often in the forms of circles, lines, flowers, or other designs. In addition to the needles themselves, some people weave coloured ribbons or laces between the needles,
- Designs created during cutting, and
- Patterns created from wax as it runs and cools over someone's body, and the intermix of colours from the different waxes as they run together or run over each other.

Because of this artistic component, most of the activities I've mentioned above can have a strong effect on a submissive beyond the activities themselves. This happens through the submissive experiencing being used as a canvas for their partner's artistic expression. This can be a powerful form of objectification where the submissive becomes merely a tool for their dominant or master to use while creating art.

Submissives can also be creative. This creativity can appear in bondage in the form of escapologist bottoms who take delight in finding new and inventive ways of escaping the bonds placed on them by their top.

Predicament bondage is an opportunity for inventiveness from both the submissive and their top. For the top, it is by means of constant refinement of the bondage through devising new knots, new angles, and new positions. The cleverness of the situation, rather than the appearance, is important. For the submissive, cleverness and lateral thinking can defeat, even if only temporarily, the postural predicaments their top creates.

In D&s and M/s, masters and dominants can be creative in designing training regimes and exploring their partner. Instead of simply working or using their partner, they may look for new, challenging, unusual, and demanding exercises for their partner.

10.1 The tinkerer

When talking about art we mustn't forget the tinkerer. Just as you see in the old teen movies from the 60s where young males souped up their new cars so they could go cruising for girls, or where home handymen spent hours in their workshops building who-knows-what, or now where modern day geeks fine-tune their computer desktops or add the latest-and-greatest software to their computers, BDSM also has its tinkerers.

These are the people who use BDSM as an excuse or as a context in which to tinker or muck around with stuff. It used to be that tinkerers would fiddle around under the bonnet of their cars way back when, and then moved on to fiddling under the bonnet of their computer when cars became too complex for mortal man. Our tinkerers fiddle with different types of rope, experiment with different types of knots, devise new pinching and clamping devices out of discarded stuff, or build bondage or torture furniture in their garage.

Many forms of tinkering aren't directly connected with play. They are often done in the days or hours before or after play. Here are a few examples:

- Cleaning or conditioning ropes,

- Building nuclear-powered nipple clamps out of things found in kitchen drawers,

- Shopping for new BDSM toys,

- Constructing bondage furniture out of bent coat-hangers and duct tape,

- Kitting out a dungeon,

- Making and oiling canes,

- Reconditioning a second-hand dentist's chair,

- Designing and making corsets,

- Designing weird spanking implements from bargains bought at the local charity shop,

- Making floggers with intricate patterns of braids on the handle, and

- Seeking out and acquiring obscure BDSM tools and equipment, such as hunting down antique violet wands on eBay® and restoring them.

10.2 Collector hobbyist

A variation on the tinkerer is the collector hobbyist. These are people who collect things. Some collectors look for particular types of BDSM tools, equipment, or gadgets. They might be fascinated by flogging and look out for floggers with tails made out of unusual material, or floggers of unusual designs, or specially-designed, one-off, custom-made floggers. My aunt used to collect salt and pepper shakers from around the world, but this probably isn't relevant.

Some collector hobbyists collect activities. They try to discover, or invent, as many different activities as possible so they can try them all, such as tree-top wax play or Push-The-Peanut.

10.3 Collecting tools, equipment and gadgets

Whenever I think about people who collect BDSM paraphernalia I think of my above-mentioned aunt or of another person I know who collects things shaped like owls. Anyway... for whatever reason, some BDSM people like to collect things based on a theme. Sometimes the collections are useful, sometimes not. Some of the things they collect include:

- Floggers, particularly handcrafted floggers or floggers made from unusual materials (human hair, fishing line, octopus nostril hair, the web of the South American hip-hop spider, etc.),

- Candles from different countries and cultures, or candles made of different types of wax, or with different types of dyes,

- Knives of different shapes and sizes, with and without serrated blades, for cutting and for mind fucks,

- Hypodermic needle tips of various lengths, bores, and different colours for piercing and creating patterns,

Artists and tinkerers

- Handcuffs, though having more than one pair of handcuffs begs the question: how many hands does your submissive have?
- Rope of different thicknesses, different materials (hemp, nylon, cotton, plastic, natural fibre, etc.), different textures, different colours, different stiffnesses,
- Pegs, clamps, pincers, and tweezers,
- Attachments for a violet wand.

Collecting often goes hand-in-hand with large amounts of time spent sorting, polishing, and discussing the collections with other people.

10.4 Collecting activities

In book two of this series, *BDSM Relationships - How They Work*, I have a chapter containing lists of all sorts of BDSM activities. My lists are intended to be used to enrich your BDSM relationship by helping you discover new activities to share with your partner. Some people however, take such lists as challenges and want to be able to say they've tried every single activity. These people are activity collectors. Their hobby is to find and try everything they can. It's usually not that they need to do so, or that they have some hidden and unsatisfied urge which drives them to try ever more challenging or difficult activities. No. It's often just the same as collecting charms on a charm bracelet or collecting stamps[1] is for other people. It adds a little extra

---
[1] I wonder if foot fetishists collect stamps? [pun intended]

interest to what they do and gives them something to display at show-and-tell or to talk about at parties.

10.5 Show and tell

This is one important—but often unspoken—aspect of tinkering. Taking your latest-and-greatest flogger, fucking machine, or amazing hand-woven rope acquisition from the Upper Kalahari to the next play party or BDSM social event and showing it around can be just as important in some ways as using it on your partner. Many creative aspects of BDSM stand up well both as ways of demonstrating your passion and enthusiasm to others, and as chances to get your ego fluffed up a little by the oohs and ahs of those who admire either your handiwork or your diligence at seeking out obscure treasures.

10.6 Incompatibility

While tinkering and art can happen in a BDSM context, it can be boring, annoying, or distracting if you're trying to have a scene with your partner and instead of helping you to immerse yourself in the experience they're trying to get a difficult knot just right or they're trying to get the molten wax to pool in a certain way.

They may have a need to be creative sometimes, and you do need to ensure that they have these opportunities. But equally, you will have your own needs which perhaps aren't met while they're being creative. While there might be an element of incompatibility in this, there's no reason why you can't both take

Artists and tinkerers

turns at being, on one hand, creative or being the canvas and, on the other, enjoying full-on BDSM.

If you find their tinkering to be getting in the way sometimes, say so. Don't be brutal about it, but try to discuss it. Maybe suggest a compromise where you dedicate some agreed sessions to art and some to needs-meeting.

And if you're a tinkerer, or if you like to use your BDSM play sessions as times to be artistic, make sure you let your partner know and make sure you both agree on the times when art will be the focus or when, instead, savage bloodletting will.

10.7 Artistry

Before finishing off this topic I'd like to just briefly list a few activities in which creative expression can play a significant, even if not obvious, part:

- Rope bondage:
    - Particularly in forms of bondage such as Shibari where the goal is to create a work of art combining the rope itself, the knots, their placement, and the subject, and
    - Where the position or posture of the tied subject is expressive, such as being a statement of vulnerability or eroticism.

- Cutting - where the person being cut serves as a canvas on which the person doing the cutting creates their designs. The designs may be permanent, leaving a scar when healed, or temporary, healing completely and leaving no scar.

- Branding - where designs are burned, using intense heat or cold, into the flesh of your partner.

- Piercing - where patterns of needles or skewers are created in the flesh of your partner.

- Caning, whipping, and sometimes flogging - where the strokes leave patterns of lines on the back, buttocks, or thighs of your partner.

- Erotic stimulation - some see the use of various implements, BDSM or otherwise, to erotically stimulate their partner as an art form, with their partner's orgasm at the end being the climax of their particular artistic spectacular.

10.8 Conclusion

Perhaps the most important goal of tinkering and art is this exercise of creativity. The intensity and primality of some forms of BDSM play—such as flogging, caning, sex play, pain play, and so on—can preclude creativity and often just require strength, physical endurance, or just raw animal passion. On the other hand, tinkering, collecting, and art provide what can be an important outlet for creative juices while still remaining in a BDSM context, or while remaining within the context of a BDSM relationship with your partner.

Tinkering should be supported and encouraged. Always be ready to view what your partner has tinkered and be ready to support

Artists and tinkerers

them and what they've done. Encourage them to show it and to try it out. Contribute and offer suggestions, and never diminish it or put it or them down in any way, even if you think what they've done is wacky.

Often the results of these inclinations aren't necessarily intended to be entirely practical or useful, but are instead simply creative expressions. Keep this in mind.

Chapter 11

Assembling the pieces

Knowing how to execute a BDSM activity with technical proficiency is often easy to learn. There are many books around on the practical side of BDSM. Many BDSM enthusiast groups run workshops on the most common forms of play, and if you happen to come across someone doing something new or interesting at a BDSM play party, there's a good chance that if you wait until they're finished and then ask them about it that they'll give you some tips.

But underlying these practical displays and these mechanical interactions with the people with whom we do our BDSM is often a need to have some sort of relationship with them. While there are some people who look for anonymous BDSM encounters to get simple needs met—such as for basic pain or humiliation—many of us look for something more profound, and for that we often need to have a partner who we trust, who knows us, and with whom we can develop something more than what an anonymous encounter or a quickie at a BDSM play party permits.

The nature of BDSM relationships—what goes into them and what we get out of them—is often not clear or easy to grasp, but the fact is that many of us look for a regular partner even though on the surface it looks like all we might do with them is the same sort of activity we can get anonymously at a BDSM play party or at a professional BDSM establishment or bondage parlour. The actual role the relationship has in these explorations is not something we always understand.

It can be tempting to compare BDSM relationships to vanilla relationships, but as I noted at the beginning of this book there's a fundamental difference in that in a BDSM relationship the BDSM part means that we do things *to* our partners, rather than merely *with* them as is the case for vanilla relationships. This *doing to* is what allows us to penetrate our partners, to cause them to feel something coming from us. When that goes away, so does the BDSM and we are left either with a vanilla relationship or with nothing at all.

I've tried to show in the preceding chapters that there's more that we can and do get out of BDSM when we engage a partner while doing so. When we have a foundation of trust, when we learn what our particular partners need and respond to, and when they know us, then we can open ourselves up to being engaged by them. We can also target what we do and how we react specifically to them, not just to An Average Submissive or to An Average Dominant. This means that what we share is more likely to hit the mark and be more effective than just by doing "standard moves".

Importantly in all this, BDSM is often a form of self-expression which we expose or show with our partners. It might take a primal, physical, or even sexual form, and it can be critical to recognise this when it is the case. Being able to be ourselves with our partner—be they dominant or submissive, master or slave, top or bottom—can be one of the most important things which a BDSM relationship provides, and it might be that the physical side of BDSM is just a context which allows this to occur. Focussing on the physical activities, on their technical execution, can take away from the personal and people needs which are the real purpose for What It Is That We Do.

In book two of this series, *BDSM Relationships - How They Work*, I'll be looking at practical techniques and strategies for developing and maintaining a BDSM relationship. Then, in book three, *BDSM Relationships - Pitfalls and Obstacles*, I'll be looking at many of the problems which can occur trying to keep and maintain a long-term BDSM relationship and at what you can do to avoid or overcome them.

Bibliography

[ANTONIOU1995] Antoniou, Laura. *Laura, Leather, and Life*. Lecture at Crossroads Learning Center, Seattle, Washington, November 1995

[GRANDIN1992] Grandin, Temple. *Calming Effects of Deep Touch Pressure in Patients with Autistic Disorder, College Students, and Animals*. Journal of Child and Adolescent Psychopharmacology, volume 2, no. 1, pages 63 – 72, 1992. ISSN 1044-5463

[HILL1996] Hill, Craig A. and Preston, Leslie K. *Individual Differences in the Experience of Sexual Motivation: Theory and Measurements of Dispositional Sexual Motives*. The Journal of Sex Research, volume 33, no. 1, pages 27 – 45, 1996. ISSN 0022-4499

[KRAUSS1987] Krauss, Kirsten E. *The Effects of Deep Pressure Touch on Anxiety*. The American Journal of Occupational Therapy, vol-

	ume 41, no. 6, pages 366 – 373, 1987. ISSN 0272-9490
[MASTERS2008]	Masters, Peter. *This Curious Human Phenomenon: An exploration of some uncommonly explored aspects of BDSM*. The Nazca Plains Corporation, 2008. ISBN 1-9346-2568-X
[MASTERS2009]	Masters, Peter. *The Control Book*. CreateSpace, 2009. ISBN 1-4421-7386-6
[MESTON2007]	Meston, Cindy M. and Buss, David M. *Why Humans Have Sex*. Archives of Sexual Behaviour, volume 36, no. 4, pages 477 – 507, 2007. ISSN 0004-0002

Glossary

24/7 — short for 24 hours a day, seven days a week. This refers to a type of D&s or M/s relationship where the two people involved always interact and engage each other in D&s or M/s terms.

BDSM — an acronym for Bondage and Discipline, Dominance and Submission, and Sadism and Masochism.

Bondage — a BDSM activity where a top, dominant, or master uses rope, chain, cuffs or any other method to physically restrain their bottom, submissive, or slave.

Bottom — a BDSM role. A bottom is the one on the receiving end during a BDSM scene such as the one being tied up, the one being struck with a flogger, etc.

Cutting — a BDSM activity using very sharp knives or scalpels to cut designs into the skin. These can be shallow cuts, usually through only a layer or two of skin and which are more for psychological effect than to be

	actually painful, through to deep cuts which bleed and leave scars.
D&s	a short-hand way to refer to dominant/submissive relationships.
Discipline	any BDSM activity involving an aspect of punishment. Typically things like bare-bottom spanking and caning fall into this category.
Dominant	a BDSM role. A dominant takes charge of some aspect of their partner's activities. This can be solely for the length of a scene, or longer term when they live together.
Dungeon	a special area reserved for BDSM scenes. Usually equipped with specialised and BDSM-adapted furniture such as spanking benches (padded, comfortable benches used during spanking scenes), wooden frames with anchor points used during rope bondage, etc.
Fire play	an activity involving fire, typically where a top applies a thin smear of a volatile liquid—such as an alcohol/water mix—to the skin of a bottom, lights the vapour above the bottom's skin, and then quickly extinguishes the flame to prevent burning.
Flogger	a type of short, multi-tail whip. Usually designed more to thud than sting, the tails are often shorter than one metre and are typically fairly wide and soft. The tails can be made of leather, rope, cord, hair, rubber, etc.

Understanding BDSM Relationships

Impact play   any BDSM activities where striking one's partner is the goal. Includes slapping, spanking, paddling, whipping, flogging, and so on.

M/s   a short-hand way to refer to Master/slave relationships.

Master   a BDSM role. A master claims ownership or rights over a slave.

Mistress   a BDSM role. Can be the female counterpart of a master, but often this role is merely a female top.

Mummification   a type of bondage in which the whole body is encased in a form of wrapping in a manner reminiscent of an egyptian mummy (with holes for breathing, of course). Most commonly the material used for wrapping is something like kitchen cling wrap because it's quick and easy to apply.

Needle play   using hypodermic needle tips to thread through the skin, genitals or nipples. Usually done for psychological effect because the needles are actually designed not to hurt (much) unless larger diameters are used. Can also be done for artistic reasons where large numbers of needles are used at one time to create patterns.

Pain play   any BDSM activities where causing sharp or dull pain is the goal. Includes caning, whipping, flogging, cutting, etc.

Paddle   a paddle similar in shape and size to a ping-pong paddle made out of wood or thick leather. Used for paddling, which is similar to spanking but is done with a paddle instead of a hand.

Glossary

UNDERSTANDING BDSM RELATIONSHIPS

Play party a type of BDSM event where people get together to engage in BDSM activities and BDSM play with each other. Usually held in a private location, such as someone's home, warehouse, loft, or other dedicated space. Rooms or areas are usually put aside for such play, while other areas are put aside for talking, socialising or eating.

Rope bondage using rope or cord to physically restrain someone partially or fully. Includes full-body bondage, hog-tying, wrist or ankle cuffs made out of rope, etc.

Scene a collected series of activities with a BDSM focus having a clearly defined start and end; hence *bondage scene* or *discipline scene*, etc. Often performed in a dungeon.

Scene is also sometimes used as a verb meaning to engage in a scene or to perform a scene. For example, *the dominant intends to scene with his submissive*.

Slave a BDSM role. A slave assigns ownership or rights over themselves to their partner.

Squick to cause to feel repulsion, to disgust.

Submissive a BDSM role. A submissive hands over control over some of their activities to their partner for the length of a scene or longer term if they live together.

Switch a person who can adopt the role of top or bottom to suit their own and their partner's needs.

Suspension   a type of rope bondage where the person being tied is first tied and is then suspended in the air from a frame or from a bolt in the ceiling.

Top   a BDSM role. A top is the one who does things to their partner, the bottom, during a scene. This could be bondage, spanking, caning, flogging, and so on.

Toys   Equipment used for BDSM play such as floggers, canes, chains, cuffs, etc.; hence *toy bag*, i.e., a bag used for carrying around BDSM equipment.

About the author

Peter Masters is a BDSM dominant and author who lives in Sydney, Australia. He has enjoyed taking control of fine women since his early twenties (which was thirty years ago) and is the author of a number of BDSM and kinky-sex-related books.

He has a website, which is more a wiki than anything else, where you can find hundreds of articles on BDSM and related topics:

```
http://www.peter-masters.com/
```

Made in the USA
Columbia, SC
19 March 2021